The Fifth Generation
The Future of Computer Technology

No. 3069
$26.95

The Fifth Generation

The Future of Computer Technology

Jeffrey Hsu and Joseph Kusnan

Published by **Windcrest Books**
FIRST EDITION/FIRST PRINTING

© 1989 by Jeffrey Hsu and Joseph Kusnan. Reproduction or publication of the content in any manner, without express permission of the publisher, is prohibited. No liability is assumed with respect to the use of the information herein. Printed in the United States of America.

Library of Congress Cataloging-in-Publication Data

Hsu, Jeffrey.
   The fifth generation : the future of computer technology / by Jeffrey Hsu and Joseph Kusnan.
     p.   cm.
   Includes index.
   ISBN 0-8036-9069-7   ISBN 0-8306-9369-6 (pbk.)
   1. Fifth generation computers.   I. Kusnan, Joseph.   II. Title.
QA76.85.H88   1989
004—dc20   89-32278
                                                                                   CIP

TAB BOOKS Inc. offers software for sale. For information and a catalog, please contact TAB Software Department, Blue Ridge Summit, PA 17294-0850.

Questions regarding the content of this book should be addressed to:

Windcrest Books
Division of TAB BOOKS Inc.
Blue Ridge Summit, PA 17294-0850

Ron Powers: Acquisitions Editor
Eileen P. Baylus: Technical Editor
Katherine Brown: Production

Dedication

This book is dedicated to all those who seek to advance the limits of computers—to those who work to produce faster, more powerful, and more versatile machines and programs for the purpose of serving—not hindering—man.

and

To Him who makes all things possible.

Contents

Preface   xi

Acknowledgments   xiii

Introduction   xvii

Part I
Fifth-Generation Research

1. ***Japan and the Fifth Generation***   3
   Japan's Research: Three Projects 4

2. ***The United States and the Fifth Generation***   11
   Government Research: The Strategic Computing Initiative 12
   Further Research 16
   Strategic Computing for Image Understanding (SCIUP) 20
   Industry 20
   In Summary 22

3. ***Europe and the Fifth Generation***   23
   Western Europe 24
   The Soviet Union and Eastern Europe 31
   East Germany 33
   Poland 34
   Hungary 34
   Czechoslovakia, Bulgaria, and Romania 34
   In Summary 34

Part II
Fifth-Generation Hardware
and Technologies

4 *Parallel Processing*   **39**
    Parallel Systems Architectures   41
    The Future of Parallel Processing   45
    Dataflow Architecture   52
    Parallel Systems Programming   54

5 *Microchips and Microchip Technologies*   **57**
    Semiconductor Technologies   59
    Optical Technologies   68
    The Josephson Junction   72
    Molecular Technologies   75

6 *Speech Recognition*   **79**
    Advantages of Speech Processing   80
    Applications   81
    Some Background: Human Speech   82
    Problems in Speech Recognition   83
    How Speech Systems Work: Initial Analysis   84
    Recognition Techniques   85
    Speech Systems and Research   86
    Existing Systems   86
    More Recent Developments   88
    In Summary   89

7 *Vision Systems*   **91**
    The Versatility of Vision   93
    Vision Systems   93
    Computer Vision Technology   93
    Machine Vision   104

8 *Robotics*   *109*
   Why Use Robots? 111
   Applications of Industrial Robots 111
   How Do Robots Work? 114
   Robot Senses and Intelligence 120

Part III
Fifth-Generation Software
and Applications

9 *Programming Languages*   *123*
   LISP 124
   PROLOG 136
   Other Languages 140
   In Summary 142

10 *Natural Language*   *143*
   Natural Language Understanding 146
   Summary 154

11 *Expert Systems*   *155*
   Why Use Expert Systems? 157
   Structure of Expert Systems 159
   What Tasks Can Expert Systems Perform? 160
   Medical Expert Systems 162
   Geology Expert Systems 164
   Chemistry Expert Systems 165
   Computer Expert Systems 165
   Electronics Expert Systems 165
   Engineering Expert Systems 166
   Military Expert Systems 166
   Knowledge Representation 167

Expert Systems Tools   171
Building an Expert System   173
Expert Systems Research   175

Index   **177**

Preface

Computing is progressing at an incredible pace! Just a few decades ago, the widespread use of computers in homes, businesses, and schools would have been thought a fantasy—an impossibility and wishful thinking. Mammoth machines that once filled rooms with scores of vacuum tubes or transistors now can be had on a small fingernail-sized sliver of silicon, and purchased at the corner store.

Advances in computing will make even today's most advanced computers obsolete within a few years, replaced by even more powerful systems, capable not only of fast computation, but of running many programs at the same time, understanding speech, "seeing objects," performing dozens of physical tasks, and making decisions about complex problems that would take years for people to solve. The goal of a truly "intelligent computer" is not far off, and scientists are making strides towards that goal every day.

The goal of this book is to present a concise, yet comprehensive, look at the latest developments in computing research and technology. It will focus on research being done both here and in locations around the world, on hardware technology advances, and new developments that have been made in software and applications. There have been many books on artificial intelligence, and a few on "the fifth generation," however they fall into one of two groups: advanced textbooks on the theories and principles behind these new technologies, and very basic overviews of AI and "fascinating developments" type books. This book is designed to bridge the gap between these extremes and present a clear, readable account of the applications, research, and technologies that comprise the fifth generation.

You will read about the announcement of the fifth generation project by Japan, the response by the Americans, British, and Europeans, and a host of fifth-generation technologies including parallel processing, natural language, robotics, vision systems, speech, and expert systems. There are illustrations and photos that will show you what these technologies are like, and how they work.

We hope that you enjoy this exploration into the world of computers and cutting-edge technologies. We would be pleased to hear from you if you have any questions, comments, and suggestions concerning this book, or anything else that would you would like to discuss. Please write to us at P.O. Box 263, Pine Brook, NJ 07058.

Acknowledgments

We wish to thank the following for their help in making this book a reality:

Ron Powers, our editor at TAB, for his confidence in our project and his help along the long path of writing this book.

Ray Collins, Steve Fitzgerald, Bob Ostrander, Teresa Dingle, and the others at TAB who helped make this an enjoyable experience.

Thanks go to all the publishers, software companies, agencies, and other firms that provided copies of books, software, and materials for our review. Thanks also to those who provided the photographs that are included in this book.

The Fifth Generation
The Future of Computer Technology

Introduction

Progress is being made in computers at an amazing pace. Multifold advances in computing technology are springing forth every few years, and the evolution of computers has come a long way in the past few decades. In fact, the entire field of computing systems has spanned four generations, and is moving into the fifth.

The first generation of computers, beginning around the end of World War II, and continuing until around the year 1957, included computers that used vacuum tubes, drum memories, and programming in machine code. Computers at that time were mammoth machines that did not have the power of our present day desktop microcomputers.

The second generation began around 1957 and lasted until about 1963. In that era, transistors were used in lieu of vacuum tubes, and magnetic core memories were used to store information. High-level languages were developed so programmers could be spared the torture of working with op codes and binary digits. Computers were improving, but still remained out of the reach of most people.

The third generation, stretching from 1963 until around 1971, featured the use of integrated circuits, semiconductor memory, and magnetic disk storage, and the development of minicomputer systems. New operating systems, virtual memory, and timesharing were the new software advancements made during this period.

The fourth generation, lasting from the early 1970s to the end of the 1980s, is the generation we are in right now; however we are rapidly moving toward the fifth. The advent of the microprocessor made computers easily accessible to a wide segment of the population, and developments in very large scale integration (VLSI), networking, and improved memories, as well as database management systems and advanced languages, are all benefits of the fourth generation.

Now we come to the fifth generation—the subject of this book, and a vast uncharted frontier that lies before us. Never before have computers reached such levels as in the fifth generation, with smaller, faster microchips, parallel processors, new computer architectures, rapid advances in knowledge-based and expert systems, natural language processing, and advanced software concepts.

In this book, you will be able to explore the reaches of computing technology from the research, hardware, and software viewpoints. In addition, diagrams and illustrations will enable you to see for yourself how these technologies and software work. You will be amazed by how far these technologies have come from the days of the ENIAC, Mark IV, and other early systems. You will also realize the power that is contained within your desktop computer, and understand why, in a few years, desktop computers with the power of today's mainframes will be a reality.

The book is arranged into several sections, and the following is an overview to the book as a whole.

Fifth-Generation Research is the first major section of the book, and covers the research that is being done in major artificial intelligence areas around the world.

Japan and the Fifth Generation describes the development of Japan's fifth generation project: what the goals of the Japanese are, what they have accomplished, and how they have influenced the entire world with their ideas for a fifth generation computer.

The United States and the Fifth Generation describes how the Americans have competed with Japan to develop cutting-edge technologies on their own, including the Pilot's Associate, the Autonomous Land Vehicle, the ALBM, new computer architectures, natural language and speech systems, and optical technologies.

The Fifth Generation and Europe describes work being done on the British Isles through the Alvey program, the European cooperative ESPRIT, and the state of computer technology in Eastern Europe and the Soviet Union.

Fifth-Generation Hardware and Technologies discusses various technologies that are important in the fifth generation, including parallel processing, microchips, speech, vision, and the developments in robotics.

Parallel Processing addresses the very real benefits of parallel processing, of thousands of processors working together to solve problems, and the various methods that have been used to produce truly parallel computers.

Microchips and Microchip Technologies encompass a wide range of fields, including advanced semiconductors, the HEMT, ballistic transistors, gallium arsenide, photolithography, wafer-scale integration, optical technologies, transphasors, Josephson junctions, and molecular technologies.

Speech Processing discusses the goal for a listening and speaking computer, and the barriers that stand in the way. The complexities of understanding spoken speech and of recognition by computers are covered, as well as some revolutionary concepts and products that have appeared, including the Hearsay II, IBMs Voice Typewriter, and others.

Vision Systems covers the ever important field of vision systems and how human vision is represented and interpreted by a computer. It also describes some of the new systems that have been developed to interpret images, and in a sense can "see" much like a human does.

Robotics covers the entire realm of robotics, including its lore and history, the uses for which robots have been designated over the years, the structure of robots, and the direction toward which robotics is headed.

Fifth-Generation Software and Applications describes the advances in the areas of software, programming, and applications areas, which are important parts of the fifth generation. Included are expert systems, natural language, and programming languages.

Programming Languages explores the world of computer programming for artificial intelligence, including the two major ones, LISP and PROLOG, both of which are discussed in depth. The section also covers the various lesser-known languages, including SMALLTALK, SAIL, PLANNER, LOOPS, and FRL.

Natural Language describes the work that is being done to achieve one of the most sought-after goals in computing: creation of a computer that can understand the English language and work fluently with English, rather than numbers, commands, or other means. The techniques, problems, and research in this area are discussed.

Expert Systems is one of the most important parts of the fifth generation, existing at the center of the intense new interest in knowledge engineering and making programs more intelligent. It discusses what expert systems are all about, why we should develop more expert systems, how they are put together, and what tasks they have been set up to solve. It also includes knowledge representation concepts, expert system tools, building of an expert system, and research in this area.

This book is must reading if you want to know what is happening right now, around the world, in terms of advances being made in the rapidly growing world of computing. Think about it—computers are everywhere, and will continue to be dominant in our lives as we enter the 21st century. There is nothing more important than to understand and know what these machines of the future are about, and how we can use them to forge ahead into the unknown.

Part I
Fifth-Generation Research

Chapter 1
Japan and the Fifth Generation

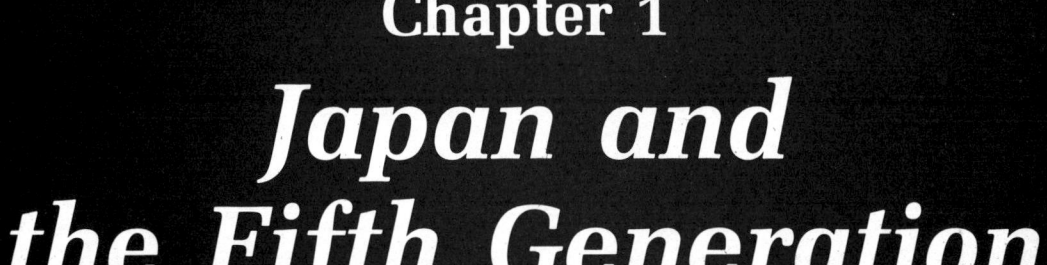

On October 19, 1981, at the International Conference on the Fifth Generation Computer in Tokyo, the Fifth-Generation Computer Project was announced. This was the first announcement to the world of the concept of a fifth-generation computer, and was the beginning of the "new wave" of computing that is the subject of this book.

Without a doubt, the Japanese are the ones who started the entire realm of fifth-generation computing. It was their work in this field that brought the entire world to the realization that the time had come for work on revolutionary technologies and ultrahigh-speed computing systems. Their goal was to dominate the world in terms of research on the various technologies involved in the fifth generation, and to establish themselves as the world leader in computer science research.

The purpose of this chapter is to provide an overview of the research that Japan is doing in the fifth generation, starting from the early beginnings all the way to the new developments that are planned for the future. The Japanese set the pace for fifth-generation research around the world, and without them, worldwide progress in artificial intelligence would proceed at a much slower pace.

Japan's Research: Three Projects

Japanese research in the fifth generation is run under the auspices of the government, and has a clearly defined direction and goal. The Japanese have organized their work into three main national projects: the Superspeed Computer Project, the Next-Generation Industries Project, and last, but certainly not least, the Fifth-Generation Computer Project.

Superspeed Computer Project

The Superspeed Computer Project is concerned with the development of ultrafast computers. Begun in 1981 and continuing past 1989, the project has received $100 million in funding from the Ministry of International Trade and Industry. Major Japanese firms that are participating in the project include what is known as the "Big Six": Fujitsu, Hitachi, NEC, Mitsubishi, Oki, and Toshiba. The goal is to produce a computer that can perform 10 million floating-point operations per second, as well as contain a main memory of 1 billion bytes. The plan calls for a prototype to be built sometime in the late 1980s.

The Next-Generation Industries Project

The Next-Generation Industries Project is in general much broader in scope than the preceding project, and concentrates on a wide variety of goals, including special components for high-speed computers, structures based on three dimensions, and computing components designed for use in extreme and hostile environments. The project will run through the 1980s and be funded at close to $500 million.

Fifth-Generation Computer Project

The Fifth-Generation Computer Project is of the greatest interest to us, and is the subject of the remainder of this chapter. It is a wide-reaching program that encompasses many areas of computing and has many ambitious goals. Some of the areas covered include problem-solving and inference, knowledge-base management, and intelligent interfaces.

Although the project officially began in 1982, the idea for the fifth-generation computer began as early as 1979. At that time, the Ministry of International Trade and Industry (MITI) requested a survey from Japan's Information Processing Development Association (JIPDEC) about a fifth-generation computer. Although at the time Japan's electronic industry was progressing well and quality goods were being offered for export, Japan was not certain what its direction should be in terms of computing research for the 1980s and 1990s. The idea was for a two-year study to evaluate the state of society, both in Japan and abroad, of computing needs, research, and response. This included a look at whether there were any problems that required national attention, and any approaches that needed to be taken in regard to research.

A committee was formed to perform the study, and it was chaired by the late Tohru Moto-oka of Tokyo University. There were three main areas—or special-interest groups—that were studied, and each was headed by an expert in the field. Hajime Karatsu, associated at that time with the Matsushita Tsushin Company, headed the group that studied the type of computer that the society of the 1990s would require. In order to determine the social environment that would likely exist in the future, Karatsu and the other members of this "Systems Technology Group" worked with and participated with banks, computer users, manufacturers, trading companies, and others to reach some viable conclusion. The entire group consisted of 10 major members, as well as 53 in the "working group" associated with it.

To study computer technology architecture, a group led by Hideo Aiso, professor of electrical engineering at Keio University, was formed. It consisted of 12 main members and 12 working members. Finally, a basic theory group, headed by Kazuhiro Fuchi, pattern information director at the Electrotechnical laboratory, studied fundamental research questions in cooperation with various mathematicians, linguists, and other professionals. There were 13 main members, and 48 in the working group.

Over the two-year survey period, a total of more than 100 people were working on various aspects of the survey, with over 100 meetings and a lot of hours expended toward deciding upon the direction and goals of their fifth-generation computer.

Finally, on October 19, 1981, at the International Conference on the Fifth-Generation Computer, held in Tokyo, the Fifth-Generation Computer Project was announced.

The entire project would be headed by Tohru Moto-oka and Kazuhiro Fuchi, and would be a 10-year program to be started officially in April 1982. The Institute of New Generation Computer Technology (ICOT) would provide funding in the form of $20 million to $30 million, and Japanese companies would contribute their time and resources to the project as well.

At the conference, more than 80 participants were from overseas, and in fact both T. Moto-oka and K. Fuchi spent time traveling to the United States, Great Britain, Germany, and France discussing the project. The two heads of the project met with such experts as Feigenbaum and Dertouzos in the United States and Colmeraur in France.

International Response One of the goals of the projects was to elicit international cooperation, and the announcement of the plans brought about reactions from various parts of the world. The major countries involved in research in this area included Great Britain, the United States, Western European nations, and others, and they all had their own reactions to Japan's plans.

In Britain, a committee was set up to determine the British response to the fifth generation. This committee was headed by John Alvey from British Telecom, and the report, released in the fall of the following year, was known as the Alvey Report. The results of this report showed that the British government should set aside funds for computer research and become more active in this area. The initial budget provided for this research was in the neighborhood of $500 million.

The British project covered a wide range of areas, including knowledge processing, VLSI, man-machine interfaces, and other applications and developments at both universities and industry. The project was truly national in nature, and included participation by the Department of Education, Department of Trade and Industry, and the Department of Defense.

On the other side of the Atlantic, the Americans also had their own projects in the works, including work by both the government and private industry. A research consortium known as Microelectronics and Computer Technology (MCC) was set up, with the participation of manufacturers of computers and semiconductors, including Control Data. The Defense Applied Research Projects Agency (DARPA) of the Department of Defense also, some time later, started work on a strategic programming research program, which included some attention to artificial intelligence. One hundred billion dollars was devoted to this research.

In Europe, the Germans, French, and European Community also had their own plans. West Germany committed a national budget to developing leading edge technology, especially in the areas of knowledge-based systems and advanced computer architectures. Some 3.5 million deutsche marks were devoted initially to the project.

A committee was set up in France to study information processing, known as Systemes Informatiques de la Connaissance (SICO) at the National Information Processing Laboratory (INRIA).

Finally, the European Community formulated a plan known as European Strategic Plan for Research in Information Technology (ESPRIT) which has as its focus 12 large computer companies located throughout Europe. These companies were located in Great Britain, France, Germany, Italy, and the Netherlands. The goal was to prevent Europe from lagging behind Japan and the United States in computing research by stimulating cooperative effort between European nations. Among the participants are Siemens of West Germany, Bull from France, and ICL from Great Britain.

Research Areas The main focus of the Fifth-Generation Computer Project at the research lab was on developing architectures and languages for concurrent symbolic computation. Other labs were set to work on expert systems, pattern recognition, and various related areas. In summary, the Fifth-Generation Project would focus on the following research areas:

- ☐ VLSI
- ☐ Advanced architectures
- ☐ Software systems
- ☐ Artificial intelligence

More specifically, the goal of the project was to develop computer systems with three main parts, including a problem-solving/inference base, a knowledge-based system, and an intelligent user interface. The time frame for this program was specified as having an initial, intermediate, and final phase, comprising a total of 10 years.

The initial phase would run for three years and would focus on accumulating and evaluating the previous research in the field up to that time, with attention to knowledge and information processing. A serial relational database will be the knowledge base in this initial phase.

The intermediate phase, lasting four years, would try to improve on this research and make what modifications and expansions were necessary. Inference systems and knowledge bases would be the focus of the work, with the result being a parallel knowledge base.

The final phase would look into construction of a total system that would use the techniques and knowledge learned in the previous stages. The resulting knowledge-based computer would combine the database machine with the inference machine.

What have the results of the research been so far, and what have they accomplished? In some areas, the results have perhaps not been as extensive as originally planned. Funding for the project did not reach the levels originally planned, and some projects such as VLSI were dropped. A 100,000-word lexicon known as the Electronic Dictionary, originally planned as a demonstration of the Fifth-Generation Project, eventually evolved into an endeavor separate from the main project.

The emphasis on PROLOG and programming using logic has been one of the key focus points of the Japanese project, however it might not end up to be the best way to proceed, compared to other areas. In fact, they have been working with other related approaches, such as guarded horn clauses, another form of logic programming that attempts to simplify the transition to parallel programming. Also, the Japanese have turned their efforts mainly in the areas of logic machines and operating systems.

One important project, the PSI logic-programming machine, did not meet earlier expectations. Developed by Mitsubishi Electric, Oki Electric Industry Company, and ICOT, the PSI machine was considered generally inferior to LISP workstations developed in the United States. However, it is a powerful machine, and its latest version, PSI 2, has a 320 megabyte memory, high-speed VLSI implementation, and CMOS technology, allowing it to deal with large-scale problems. ICOT is working on a network linking up 16 to 64 PSI machines into a high-speed system.

Other projects that are currently in the works include a knowledge-based machine, which is a special-purpose computer designed to retrieve information from large knowledge bases. The goal, by the early 1990s, is to achieve a speed of 1 billion logical inferences per second (LIPs).

Another project is DELTA, a relational database management machine that consists of four linked dual-processor elements, and can store up to 20 billion facts. The machine is specially designed to manage the storage and retrieval of information.

In summary, the Japanese have been the originators and pioneers in the field of fifth-generation computer research. Their work has not only made significant advances in the areas of computing technology, but has brought the world to the realization that fifth-generation computers are feasible, possible, and worthy of further time, money, and effort.

Chapter 2
The United States and the Fifth Generation

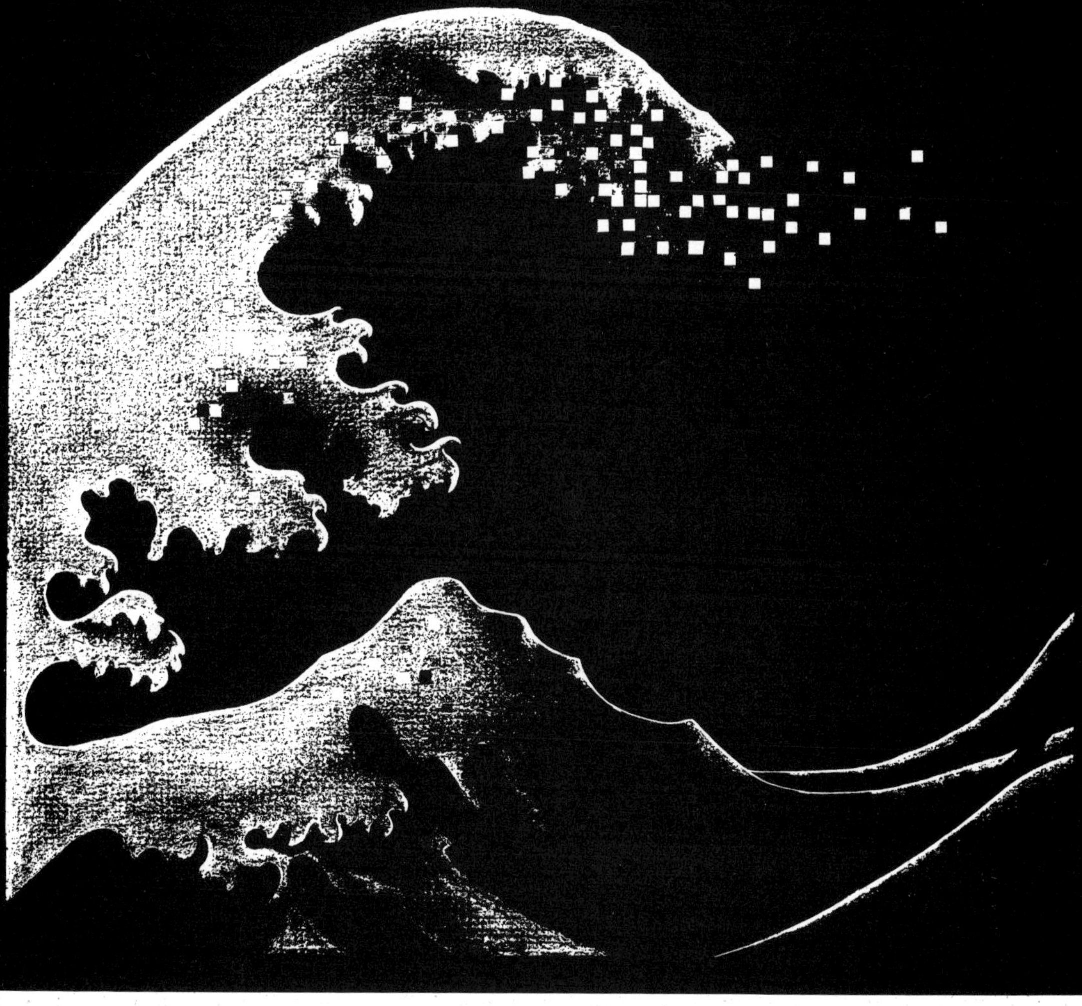

The United States is a powerful challenger of Japan in the fifth-generation race. Ambitious programs, sponsored by both the government and industry, are making significant advances in the field of artificial intelligence and fifth-generation research.

The subject is of much interest in newspapers, magazines, and in scholarly circles. American research has encompassed a wide variety of technologies, including microelectronics, knowledge-based systems, speech and natural-language recognition, Computer-Assisted Design (CAD), parallel processing, database management, and human factors.

The purpose of this chapter is to explore the research being done in these and other areas, with emphasis on the government-sponsored Strategic Computing Initiative (SCI) and the Strategic Computing for Image Understanding (SCIUP), as well as work done by Microcomputer and Computer Technology (MCC), Semiconductor Research Corporation (SRC), and other firms.

Government Research: The Strategic Computing Initiative

SCI was announced in 1983 and begun in 1984 as a government-sponsored program for research in parallel computer architectures and machine intelligence. This is a large-scale project that encompasses many parts, and is funded by the Defense Advanced Research Projects Agency (DARPA). In 1984, $1 billion was allocated to the project, distributed over a period of ten years. DARPA and other offices of the government have been in support of artificial intelligence projects for some time, including funding over the past 20 years and providing some 90 percent of the funding for research in these fields.

The areas covered in this project include microelectronics advancements and applications for military and defense use, as well as various forms of machine intelligence, including knowledge-based systems, vi-

5. Program development
6. Program demonstration
7. Testing
8. Evaluation

Pilot's Associate is a sophisticated program, encompassing five separate modules. Each has its own specific function and will be constructed in a unique way. The five modules are as follows:

The first module is *flight avionics*. This takes care of fuel, weapons status, navigation, and related functions. In conventional airplanes, these tasks usually are the responsibility of the "back seater" in multiple-crew airplanes. This module can be of great help whenever a crucial situation occurs, and the crew requires constant, accurate knowledge of the status of these resources. For instance, weapons supplies and status require constant monitoring for supply, readiness, and the correct figures for targeting and configuration. The Pilot's Associate keeps track of these multiple factors on a constant, moment-by-moment basis, and will inform the crew of any changes and emergency situations.

The second module is directed toward *mission and flight planning*. While missions are planned in advance, changes and surprises that might occur during combat can require large-scale modifications. This replanning is usually quite complex and usually cannot be considered to the necessary full extent now with conventional means. The use of this module of the Pilot's Associate will take into account every scenario and opportunity and use its knowledge to come up with viable suggestions and strategies. It will even consider such factors as weather, damage to the aircraft, and changes in combat support.

The third module is directed toward *threat assessment*. It is a program that will analyze the current combat situation and supply tactics on an immediate basis. The Pilot's Associate, through this module, can actually control the airplane, and through various conceptual goals given to it by the "mission commander" (pilot), the computer can execute these instructions and actually fly the plane.

The benefit of an aircraft controlled by a computer is the speed with which it can react to sudden changes and problems (however, control can be switched back to manual if necessary). These technologies allow humans to work with and fly more sophisticated and complex aircraft, which require the consideration of a multitude of variables and possible decisions.

sion, speech recognition, natural language, and computational mathematics.

The focus on the work is on three applications for military use—the Pilot's Associate, the Autonomous Land Vehicle, and the Air-Land Battle Management System (ALBM). The SCI project is considered very important, because it lays the groundwork for the Strategic Defense Initiative (SDI), and all the sophisticated technologies needed for its operation. Despite the practical uses of any particular project within the program, the main goal is to automate various intelligent functions, and make advances in software that can work with advanced hardware for various applications needs. At the present time, however, progress in the program is behind schedule, and budget cuts have hindered its further development. The constant need for more funding has not yet been fully met. Various delays and problems, including the lengthening of the process for signing on contractors from 3 months to 1 year, have occurred.

Pilot's Associate

The Pilot's Associate, the first of the three major military applications, is an expert system for military combat aircraft. This system is designed to remove pilots from many of the low-level functions and operations of flight, allowing them to concentrate more on high-level decisions and strategy. The plan that was mapped out is as follows: two phase one contracts were awarded to McDonnell Douglas and Lockheed-Georgia for the development of the system, each of which would lead to the design of a prototype. This "phase one" would last from February 1986 until 1988, a total of about 120 "worker-years."

Following that, phase two would take place. This includes a review of the prototype design, a full mission simulation in 1990, and complete testing and evaluation by both civilian and military pilots.

The $24.1 million project is broken down into eight major "milestones," which would be measures of the progress in this project. These milestones are:

1. Specification of program requirements
2. Design of the knowledge base
3. Detailed design
4. Module development

The next module controls *tactical evolution*, which includes the tasks of mission-planning and threat-assessment. It is designed to monitor and allocate the aircraft's resources based on the basic mission goal, priorities, and the likely probability of success for various choices.

The final module is a *pilot-system interface*, which allows the pilot to communicate with the system in an efficient and productive manner. It will function much like an operating system, a basis for all the other programs. It can correlate and work with all the other modules and data. Two important parts of this interface are speech recognition and natural language. It must be able to understand speech of various intonations, accents, and styles, especially evident when the combat situation changes. Natural language is important because the pilot and others working with the system need to communicate quickly and naturally with the system, and also have every message understood perfectly during crucial situations. It must also be able to distinguish between sensible and inappropriate orders from the pilot, especially when a human is subject to extreme stress, injury, or lack of oxygen. This fifth module is considered to be a most important part of the system, yet challenging to design and implement.

The ultimate result of the Pilot's Associate is an airplane that requires no crew.

Autonomous Land Vehicle

Using techniques developed from supercomputers, expert systems, machine vision, and sensor technologies, DARPA is working on a project, described to be a "brilliant" weapon system. The vehicle, known as an ALV, is able to travel a self-planned route over varied terrain, avoid obstacles, and make modifications to its route if obstructed in its path. It can decide on objectives as the field conditions change.

Using these technologies, DARPA is planning an Army Advanced Ground Vehicle Technology program designed to increase soldier effectiveness many times over. Also, there are plans to use this technology to help reduce crew size in the M-1 Battle Tank.

The main contractor for this project is Martin Marietta, and some progress has been made. However, human interfaces is an area where further development is needed. The current model can travel up to 17 kilometers an hour, averaging about 10 km/hr on straight paths and 3 km/hr on curves.

A major part of this technology is the ALV expert system, which is planned to have some 65,000 rules, with about 7,000 rules "firing" per second. However, at the present stage, there are only a few hundred rules and a much slower rate of firing. In any case, this should be an important new development for land combat vehicles.

Air-Land Battle Management System

Designed for use with weapon systems, the ALBM can reduce weapon system maintenance costs with self-diagnostics, and increase preparedness of these systems for battles. There are two major parts of the ALBM, the Force Requirements Expert System (FRESH) and the Combat Action Team (CAT). FRESH, developed by Texas Instruments, constantly monitors the readiness of various situations and determines the effects of changes, generates alternatives, and evaluates the effect of force changes on battlefield conditions. The CAT, developed by Carnegie-Mellon University and the Naval Ocean Systems Center, is a battle-management program that runs on a VAX minicomputer and assesses perceived enemy intent and attempts to improve performance. It is currently being used on the aircraft carrier USS Carl Vinson; however, processing is still quite slow, at 5 to 10 rules per second. The ideal speed is much higher, up to several hundred thousand rules per second. Natural language and speech capabilities are already part of the system, and other plans for CAT include a parallel processing implementation that would speed CAT to more than 1,000 rules per second.

Further Research

These three projects are important parts of the SCI, and will help improve the efficiency of our military forces and equipment. Besides these decidedly military applications, research is being done on computer architectures, natural language, speech recognition, and several other areas. The following sections will describe this research.

Computer Architectures

A great deal of progress has been made in the area of computer architectures, and one of the goals of DARPA is to make thousand-fold gains in parallel computers every 3 years. A number of major projects underway will attempt to make progress in the field.

The Connection Machine, constructed by Thinking Machines Corporation, is a system of extreme speed, eventually consisting of 65,536 processors that can solve general computational and stereo-image problems at the speed of 1 BIPS. Fluid dynamics simulations yielded speeds of 7 BIPS, about four times faster than the Cray X/MP, costing only one-sixth the price. A database query, which takes 6 hours on an IBM system and 15 minutes on a Cray X/MP, takes just 3 minutes on the Connection Machine. At this time, the most advanced system developed has about 16,000 processors working in parallel, with each being able to communicate with the others through a fast message-exchange bus. The ultimate goal is to have as many as a million microprocessors working in parallel.

The Butterfly, developed by Bolt, Bernandek, and Newman, was the first large-scale multiprocessor architecture to come out of the Strategic Computing program. This involves a series of 256 processors linked by a 4-by-4 crossbar switch, which uses the concept of packet switching to achieve crossbar communication. This can accommodate high-bandwidth packet communications, and can collect and concentrate digitized speech for DARPA's wideband satellite network. Each processor can operate up to 1 MIPS and can have between 1 and 4 megabytes of memory. The system is programmable in the C language, and the current stage of development involves a 128-node machine using commercial microprocessors.

The Warp (or programmable) Systolic Array, developed at Carnegie-Mellon, is a parallel processor that is ideal for working with special mathematical functions such as Fourier transforms. The Warp machine consists of 10 cells, each of which can process image and numerical data at a rate of 10 million operations a second, resulting in a total of 100 million operations per second in total.

Two prototypes were built in mid-1987, and were built on 15-inch PC-type boards with one MBit of memory. Further tests will result in low-level vision. These WARP systems are programmable, and interface with conventional host computers. The language is Common LISP. Each cell costs about $30,000.

The successor to this system is the iWARP, which offers increased performance with reduced costs and size. It consists of 72 cells, capable of 16 million operations per second per cell. Built on boards measuring only 2 by 4 inches, with 2 MBits of memory, it is 10 times faster than the Warp, but takes up one-tenth of the space. The cost of the iWARP is in the neighborhood of $1,000 a cell.

The Mach is an operating system developed by Carnegie-Mellon designed for multiprocessor architectures. It is designed to support a wide range of environments, including workstations. There are four main "primitives" that parallel the hardware components of multiprocessors: nodes of processors, channels, packets, and memories.

Reduced-Instruction Set Computers, or RISC, are alternate ways to optimize computer performance. One project of DARPA in this area is a 200 MIPS system with a set of 32-bit gallium arsenide chips. These chips are produced by MIPS Computer Systems of Sunnyvale, California. Also, Berkeley has a RISC computer known as Spur that will run Common LISP much faster than ever possible before.

LISP machines, such as the Texas Instrument Compact LISP Machine, offer a 32-bit processor on a chip 1 centimeter square. It offers increased performance in a much smaller space, and can be used for various AI applications.

These computers just discussed are some of the major computer architectures that have been developed through the support of the government and its Strategic Computing Initiative.

Natural Language

At Bolt, Berandek, and Newman, a natural-language system has been developed that uses a database and expert system, and can understand more than 2,000 words and 700 domain concepts. In future models, the vocabulary is expected to be increased to 7,000 words and 2,500 domain concepts.

Also, Cognitive Systems of New Haven, Connecticut, has created a Tactical Computer Terminal (TCT), an interactive training aid. The system encourages the user to ask questions and enter responses, utilizing the concept of conceptual dependency.

Speech Recognition

Although the systems currently existing are somewhat slow, there is progress being made in this area. Currently, there are 200-word connected speech and speaker-independent systems; however, the response time is from 100 to 200 times the rate of spoken speech, typically 2½ to 3½ minutes for each one second phrase. It is hoped that response times could be reduced to 30 to 60 seconds, with vocabularies increased to 10,000 words.

Angel, a system developed by Carnegie-Mellon, can recognize a 250-word vocabulary at 15 times real time. Unlike other systems, it uses various algorithms that function together. It recognizes phonetic units from speech, combines them into words, and then combines the words into sentences. Custom hardware processes the speech even further.

Optical Interconnections

When super-fast multiprocessors are in use, complex and cumbersome metal wiring is not the best medium for transmitting information. Instead, optical and laser technology can be used to perform the communications necessary for the billions and trillions of instructions needed per second. Light is even more exact and precise for transmitting instructions, because it can be directed from a source over to a designated detector.

At Honeywell's Physical Sciences center in Bloomington, Michigan gallium arsenide lasers have been integrated onto 3-inch wafers capable of communicating at 250 MBit/second.

Sensors Research

Sensors are highly crucial for military needs, such as for use with missiles. Using arrays of thousands of tiny infrared sensors, specialized sensors can detect aircraft more than 100 miles away and identify it from a considerable distance as well. This is useful for missile systems such as the "fire-and-forget" type. One system under development by Northrup is a 16,384 element focal-place array made of indium antimonide (InSb), just one-thousandth inch on a side, but it can spot aircraft from 115 miles away and identify it at a range of 18.5 miles. Infrared radiation is converted into video images and displayed on a television screen in an aircraft cockpit or missile control center.

Image Analysis

DARPA and the U.S. Army have funded the Advanced Digital Radar Imagery Exploitation System (ADRIES), which focuses on image analysis research. The system locates tactical targets by using contextual information, such as terrain and gathered intelligence, using its radar capabilities. It could be considered a hybrid expert system/model-based vision system that locates, classifies, and counts tactical targets.

Strategic Computing for Image Understanding (SCIUP)

This segment of the program, sponsored by DARPA and the Central Intelligence Agency, investigates parallel processing systems, such as the Warp, Butterfly, and the Connection Machine, that have real-time image understanding applications.

The government programs for advanced computer research are ambitious and designed to serve practical applications. The programs encompass many areas of computing. The developments being made can be considered to be crucial for the development of advanced military technologies and equipment, as well as for the advancement of computer technology in general.

Industry

While all the projects previously mentioned were operated by and supervised by the government, that is not all the research being done in the United States. In industry, companies such as MCC, the SRC, and others have been instrumental in carrying out advanced research in many areas of computing.

Microcomputer and Computer Technology Corp.

MCC is a large research company based in Austin, Texas, which has a budget of some $250 million over four years, and employs close to 400 people. The company was started in 1983 when William Norris, CEO and founder of Control Data Corporation, called a meeting to explore the ways that companies, normally competitors, could combine their resources to achieve significant advances in computer technology.

When it began, MCC had 10 companies participating, and now has 20. Each company owns one share in MCC, and pays to support one of four major research areas. These shareholders get licenses and a three-year lead in commercial production of any technologies produced in areas they fund.

The first CEO of MCC was Admiral Bobby Inman, former head of the National Security Agency and deputy director of the CIA. His political connections, prestige, expertise, and concern about Japanese competition helped smooth the path through Congress for MCC concerning antitrust laws that might limit or outlaw the joint effort. He helped guide the company through the scrutiny of the Justice Department, which decided not to object to this unique business arrangement.

MCC has been involved with a wide variety of areas, including software engineering, advanced computer architectures (including parallel processing, database management, AI and knowledge-based systems, human factors technology), VLSI CAD applications, and microelectronics packaging.

Although MCC represents a joint effort between companies, the shareholder structure also tends to isolate projects. Although the sharing of information between projects would seem ideal, since a different set of companies own the results, sharing would violate the contracts and agreements that exist. Also, much of the research has been shrouded in secrecy to protect the various shareholders' advantages. These are the problems that might need to be overcome to help foster increased cooperation between companies and projects.

The last few years has brought changes to MCC. The firm has lost six shareholder companies, as well as its CEO, Bobby Inman. Grant A. Dove, the new director, took over in 1987, and moved to make MCC a more market-sensitive and flexible operation. A number of marketable products have been produced by the shareholder companies, and in general MCC believes that it is ahead of schedule.

The Advanced Computer Architecture area is being refocused on areas that promise more immediate return, and one significant development has been the Proteus expert-system shell, which uses the concepts of truth maintenance. One shareholder, Honeywell Bull, has announced a Proteus-based product that works out the placement of text and advertising graphics. The company, owned by three companies (Honeywell, Bull of France, and NEC of Japan), is not a member, but "inherited" shares from the former Honeywell Information Systems. Another of its products is a Proteus-based expert system known as Plex, which assists in the placement of various computer components on boards. Another project in the works is a tool for sales and marketing people that suggests computer configurations and pricing tradeoffs to customer.

NCR has developed a commercial system known as the NCR Design Advisor that is based on the Proteus (2.0) shell. Its function is to design custom chips. It integrates rules into a single database representing 50 man-years of chip-design experience.

The NCR Design Advisor can be used to give advice to customers concerning designing their own semicustom chips, and the designs are evaluated using a Symbolics LISP workstation. The system eliminates much of the error associated with human engineering, using its understanding and reasoning about circuit design. The system can be queried about a design and asked to explain its inferences, and will ask questions itself if any ambiguities arise. It usually will detect about two-thirds of the errors on an average chip.

Another major significant advance has been made in the area of packaging. The TAB (tape-automated bonding) process was invented for packaging high-lead count chips. Instead of being packaged in hard cases, chips can be bonded onto polymer film and mounted directly to the circuit board, enabling more to be placed in the same amount of board space. Boeing Electronics is already using this technology, with Harris and Advanced Micro Devices intending to follow suit.

Finally, there are also advances in VLSI CAD and software engineering. A CAD system using a 200,000 transistor chip has been developed. Also, Plane-Text/FIG, a hypertext system for representing design documents with multiple cross-references, is available.

MCC has made a number of advances in these areas, and certainly is a firm that is at the cutting edge of fifth-generation computing.

Semiconductor Research Corporation (SRC)

SRC is a collaborative effort to channel funds to American universities to promote semiconductor research and development. In 1982, 11 chipmakers and computer manufacturers pooled $4 million to form SRC, and now it has 36 members and supports half of the semiconductor research done in American universities. The budget is in the area of $18.4 million a year. The results of SRC has been 16 patents and 61 graduates among the students SRC has supported.

In Summary

The United States is in the forefront of computing research, and whether sponsored by the government or industry, the work being done will make significant impacts on the state of fifth-generation technology.

Chapter 3
Europe and the Fifth Generation

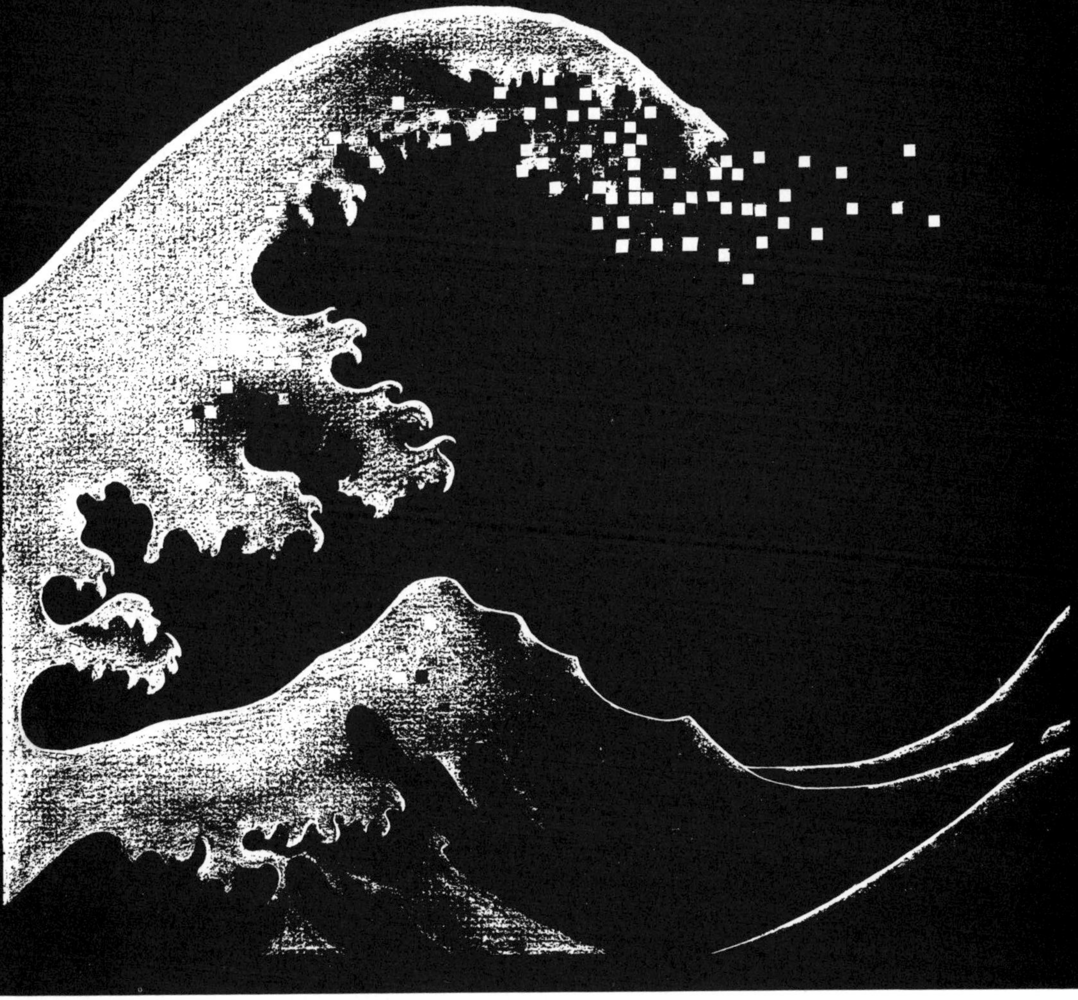

Following Japan and the United States, Europe is the third major area where fifth-generation research is going on. From the British Isles to the frontiers of the USSR, research is expanding the reaches of computing.

In contrast to the United States, for example, European research is more theoretically oriented, but there are many developments that offer direct practical applications.

Whether it is advanced microelectronics, software technology, information processing, or office automation, the Europeans have made great strides through such projects as ESPRIT, Britain's Alvey program, France's SICO program, and work in the Soviet Union and Eastern Europe.

The purpose of this chapter is to discuss and explore further the progress and developments that these projects have made.

Western Europe

European research is concentrated into several large-scale projects, sponsored by Great Britain, France, and West Germany, as well as a collaborative effort among these and various other Western European nations for ESPRIT. A number of these projects were set up in response to the Japanese conference and its announcement of work on a fifth-generation computer.

ESPRIT (Britain, Germany, France, Italy, Netherlands)

ESPRIT is a cooperative effort sponsored mainly by 12 large computer companies located in Germany, France, Italy, the Netherlands, and Great Britain, conceived both in response to the efforts being made in Japan and the United States, as well as with the hope that it could help stem the "brain-drain" that had been plaguing Europe in recent years. The goal is to create a unified program that encourages researchers to stay in Europe while at the same time break down the isolation that scientists have suffered within their respective countries. Also, a cooperative effort would eliminate the need to have nations compete and put all efforts into their national firms and programs, which is often less productive. Finally, the creation of a set of common technologies by Europe would allow them to be adopted around the world, making Europe the trendsetter and leader of computing technology standards.

The pooling of knowledge through combining both experienced research workers and academic researchers would allow the final result to have the benefits of both theory and practice, as well as the diversity of a program that in total would encompass some 200 projects, through 440 organizations, and gathering the talents of more than 3,000 people. It is quite a remarkable program, and one that has great plans for the future.

Begun in 1984, ESPRIT is conceived as a 10-year effort with funding in the neighborhood of $1.86 billion for five years as a start. It is expected to spend around $270 million a year in research and development and $70 million in artificial intelligence projects. Among the companies participating in the program are Phillips, Siemens, AEG, Nixdorf, Thomson-CSF, Bull, Olivetti, STET, ICL, and Plessey.

There are five main areas of research planned for ESPRIT:

☐ Advanced microelectronics
☐ Software technology
☐ Advanced information processing
☐ Computer-integrated manufacturing
☐ Office automation

There are numerous specific areas of interest within each category, and in general the whole project is designed to cover a broad range of interests and applications.

Advanced microelectronics deals with developments on the chip and architecture levels, including work in submicron and multilayer technologies, and the design of advanced gate structures. These all relate to hardware technologies.

It is hoped that software technologies will advance the state and level of technologies relating to large-scale software, including workstations, software engineering, portable software tools, and validation.

Advanced information processing comprises a variety of fields, including speech recognition, image processing, VLSI architectures, expert systems, and the use and development of languages, such as PROLOG and LISP.

Computer-integrated manufacturing (CIM) covers areas of interest such as CAD, robots, and image-processing systems.

Office automation, the final segment of the program, concentrates on the areas of voice input/output, flat panel displays, optical disk storage, and computerized filing systems.

The goals and areas under research by ESPRIT are certainly impressive and comprehensive, and are quite ambitious in terms of what they want to accomplish. Although only a few years have passed since the start of the program, what has ESPRIT accomplished to date, and what is the future of the program?

Even in this short period of time, ESPRIT has come up with some important advances. To ensure smooth and effective communication between the various members and offices of the research centers, a computerized information exchange network was developed. The electronic mail and conferencing network, EuroCom, has about 2,300 members throughout Europe and is funded by the EEC and participating members.

Knowledge engineering, an important part of ESPRIT research, is being studied at a special research center known as the European Computer Research Center (ECRC) located in Munich, West Germany. This center is a result of efforts by three companies, Bull of France, ICL of Britain, and Siemens of West Germany. More than 2,000 researchers work on these technologies at this center.

In terms of hardware advances, ESPRIT has created advanced .5 micrometer bipolar and CMOS integrated circuits. These new gallium-arsenide-based chips will be used on third-generation Cray supercomputers.

Another significant development is the Portable Computer Tool Environment (PCTE) interface, which is a set of common software tools that can work together easily, and is not dependent on any particular language or operating system. Currently in the public domain, it is used not only by ESPRIT, but by various other European projects.

LOKI, a computer-assisted design project is another result of ESPRIT. This project, headed by the Belgian Institute of Management and

SCS of West Germany, arranges a layer of expert systems around a conventional computer, using artificial intelligence to help ease the interaction between users and the system. The current application of this technology is in designing aircraft, and it has been successful in reducing the time for aircraft wing design from two months to two weeks.

Siemens has been working on natural language, and they are close to the release of a product known as Siconflex.

These are just a few examples of the work and advances that have resulted from the ESPRIT project. However, ESPRIT is not without its problems. The high funding levels required for the dozens of projects underway has caused several nations to reduce their support, and as a result progress toward the various goals has been reduced. Already, the loss has been calculated at 10 percent, and projects at various small companies and universities are being affected.

The original five areas of concentration have been modified, with less emphasis being placed in microelectronics, computer peripherals, and office systems. Software technology has been merged with Advanced Information Processing (AIP), and computer-integrated manufacturing with office automation. The entire approach of the project has been directed toward applications and bringing research developments to the marketplace.

Alvey (Great Britain)

In Great Britain—directly as a result of the Japanese announcement of their fifth-generation project—a group was set up to survey the situation on fifth-generation computers and artificial intelligence. John Alvey, from British Telecom, was appointed chairman, so the program is generally referred to as the Alvey program. A large number of the members of the committee are from industry. The report that came out of this committee urges the government to offer support for advanced computer research.

The program was begun in 1983, and was given funding of $525 million over a five-year period. The main areas of research to be concentrated on include VLSI, software engineering, knowledge-based systems, and man-machine interfaces. The main thrust of the program is applied research for industry, and much of the research is to be done at universities and polytechnic institutes. The program is national in form and organization, with government offices (including the Department of

Trade and Industry, Department of Education, Ministry of Defense) and almost every university and scientific institute participating. The University of Edinburgh, for example, has 12 departments participating.

A project within Alvey usually consists of four main partners, typically two or three firms working with one or two academic groups or departments. A large percentage (some 90 percent) of the research is to be conducted in academic centers, with the exception of VLSI, because the involved sophisticated equipment is not available there.

Firms with a common interest are grouped together into "Expert System Community Clubs" that would coordinate and share its knowledge in the area to create a workable expert system. Speech recognition is the subject of one such club, while risk analysis in insurance, planning, and other topics have been the subject of the others, for a total of nine clubs.

Some work has been done in VLSI, including 1.5 micrometer bipolar and CMOS circuits. In software engineering, the Aspect and Eclipse programming support environments were created, as well as the ZED specification language.

An ambitious speech project, designed to have continuous speech capabilities and an unlimited vocabulary, is currently under development. The goal is to have a system that could identify words from context rather than from matching prerecorded voice patterns. The development of a speech-recognition circuit is one of the areas being studied now. The large market for a speech product of this type is one reason why emphasis is being placed in this area.

Additional projects underway include EQUIPS, Forest, and VDM Toolset, developed at the Queen's University of Belfast and University of Edinburgh. EQUIPS is a software system that simulates the fabrication of semiconductors and is currently in use at companies such as Plessey, STC, and GEC.

Forest and VDM Toolset are toolkits and environments for software, and developed at universities in Manchester, Cambridge, Oxford, and Currey in conjunction with several major firms.

Physics is an area that has a relationship with the work at Alvey. Concepts and techniques originally developed for physics work at the engineering science department at the University of Oxford are beneficial for research in etching and depositing semiconductors. Also, at the University of Southhampton, developments related to nuclear fusion have been applied to the task of etching circuits.

A machine that records the gaps in recording heads in conventional tape recorders, another product of Alvey, has been released and is being marketed in various countries outside of Britain.

Toolkits to develop expert systems in LISP and PROLOG have been developed at the Open University, the universities of Edinburgh, and others. These are being marketed through Logica, ICL, and Systems Designers.

Parallel computer architectures is another area where advances have been made. Among the developments made in this area are chips designed to manipulate data in knowledge bases (University of Strathclyde), parallel software (Logica and Inmos), transputers that evaluate the design of parallel architectures (various firms and universities), and compilers to simulate parallel architectures.

The Flagship Project is Britain's attempt to create a parallel architecture that runs on declarative languages. These machines are able to infer answers from incomplete knowledge. The work for this project was begun at the University of Manchester and Imperial College, and will be transferred to the Alvey program.

At the University College in London, a parallel computer called graph reduction in parallel (GRIP) is being developed. Based on the concept of graph reduction, computer programs will be represented as graphs, with nodes connected by junctions. The computer will break up the program into discrete steps to keep communications between the processors at a minimum. The arrangement of the system will be 80 processor chips mounted on 10 printed circuit boards, with 5 MBytes of RAM, and will run software that will be responsive to the conditions of the data to be processed, instead of one fixed arrangement. The speed of this system will be quite improved, running at 50 MIPS rather than the 5 of present systems.

What is the future of Alvey? Close to half of the projects under Alvey had already been marketed, and hundreds of millions of pounds have been developed for the various projects. In general, the first "phase" that was planned has already been completed, and work is progressing to the second level, with more of an emphasis on applications-oriented research. The most progress has been made in the area of VLSI and software engineering; however, work on man-machine interfaces has not been quite as productive. An additional £300 million has been allocated as a future budget for Alvey, to add to the hundreds of millions already spent. Human factors will be monitored, so that there will be no neglect of how people will react to these new technologies. There will be attention to expert systems in education and speech technology. Less emphasis will be placed on software toolsets and VLSI because of costs and other problems.

Another area that Alvey is concentrating on is computer aided design, with a national database containing details of all components used to fabricate and design chips. Speed of design will be a critical factor in this area. This will be a large-scale project, with £6 million going into the software to automatically create more than one million transistor chips. The companies involved in the project include Plessey, Racal, Ferranti, Praxis, STC, ICL, and the Royal Signals and Radar Establishment. Derek Boardman, manager of the CAD project at Plessey, stated that designs that would have taken 16 years to complete can be done in six months.

The Alvey program, in summary, aims to select viable niches and concentrate on them while the world's technological giants compete on broader fronts. They hope to concentrate in areas where others, such as ESPRIT, have played down. Software will be one of Alvey's strengths, as Brian Alvey, director, put it, "... And it's just possible that the British are very good at software ... there's something about our personality that likes software."

SICO (France)

France has developed into one of the dominant nations for artificial intelligence research. Important work has been done at Systemes Informatiques de la Connaissance (SICO), a national laboratory for information research.

Work done in France includes a supercomputer known as the "Mariane Project," computer aided design and manufacturing (CAD/CAM), and software engineering for military and space applications through Electronique Serge Dassault (ESD). Developments of ESD include Dedale, an expert analog circuit fault/failure diagnostic system, an expert system designed to help engineers evaluate the layout of circuit boards, a system for quality control of integrated circuits, and an army tactical battle system.

Dedale is especially suited to expert system technology because analog circuits do not lend themselves to automatic troubleshooting based on standard algorithmic approaches. Using expert systems is much more effective and reliable. The circuit board system is useful because it can help ensure that constraints imposed by technology and operation are met prior to fabrication, using the method of evaluating heat dissipation and electronic adaptation of connections. The integrated circuit system is designed to control the quality of images through television cameras and electron microscopes. Finally, the military/strategic battle system is used in army helicopters with the Orchidee battlefield surveillance system.

Other developments include a French-English translation system for aeronautical terms, as well as a law ("Science program law") that provides for an increase in national spending in research and development. Improved support for funding and staffing of national research centers will be instituted.

West Germany

A national program exists in West Germany for research and development of data processing and information processing technologies. Knowledge-based systems and computer architectures (parallel processing) are emphasized.

The Soviet Union and Eastern Europe

Eastern Europe and the Soviet Union represent a totally different world from the West in terms of progress in computer and software technologies. The computer is thought of as a tool for Communist governments where this central, giant machine can control and manage information for the good of the state. However, the use of desktop computing systems would have the opposite effect, and when and if computer systems become widespread in the Soviet Union, the current practice of censorship would be difficult to maintain.

The state of computer technology in the USSR and Eastern Europe is at least five to ten years behind that of the West, and it is estimated that their electronics market would have to grow to five times its present size to match the level of the West. The USSR and Eastern Europe are considered to be three years behind in mainframe systems, and fifteen years behind in software development. Coupled with various economic troubles, the Eastern Bloc nations have not been able to match the investments in computers and related technologies made by Western nations. In addition, a reliance in imports has led to a decrease in the research and development in these countries. There has been a marked decline in new patents, and in the introduction of prototypes for new machines.

The Soviets are concerned about being so seriously behind technologically, both from the military and industrial viewpoints. The improvements that have been made in terms of electronics, communications, and productivity in Western nations has brought the leaders in the USSR to the realization that they have a difficult challenge ahead of them. Factories are in need of upgrades, energy and pollution problems exist, and there is a definite reliance on Western technology. The problem is compounded by the fact that the Soviets desire both the efficiency of the computer and a firm control on the information itself. In any case, the United States and Western powers have a big advantage to exploit their superiority in this area, especially in the military area.

Gorbachev has initiated a major effort to "catch up" in this area, and has elicited the support of Eastern Bloc nations to make this into a dominating policy for the Warsaw Pact alliance. Run by the International Committee for Computer Engineering (ICCE), this effort coordinates efforts in East Germany, Bulgaria, Romania, Czechoslovakia, Hungary, Poland, and the Soviet Union.

One of the committee's first goals is to put one million computers into the Soviet educational system. Training in computer science was instituted into high schools and other parts of the educational system. To improve its efforts in research, the USSR has searched throughout Eastern Europe for researchers, and also has attempted to collaborate with the United States and Japan. The organization of this program will be civilian, not military, and will be backed by $100 million in state funds. The program will deal with five major areas:

☐ Design and manufacture of VLSI microprocessors
☐ Development of parallel and multiprocessor architectures
☐ Design of operating systems to support logic programming
☐ Creation of problem-solving software
☐ Development of expert systems and application

The architect of the Soviet program is Yerengyi Velikhov, the head of the newly formed Information, Computer Technology, and Automation division of the Soviet Academy of Sciences, and considered to be one of the USSR's foremost computer scientists. Also, some 80 percent of the staff at the institute are young, having graduated from a university within the last five years.

The results so far have been uncertain. However, efforts are underway for a supercomputer known as the "Hypertron." The 1986-1990 Five-Year Plan calls for a determined effort to acquire Western technology. Restrictions on exports to Eastern Bloc nations have been eased, computer and electronics firms are allowed to have offices in the Soviet Union, and in general the flow of technology in the USSR has been encouraged rather than restricted.

There also are many problems associated with the desire for technological advances in the Soviet Union. The quality of the telephone system is poor, so it is unreliable for computer data transmission, and is still not available in many homes and locations. While in the United States the average is about 76 phones per 100 people, in Eastern Bloc nations the average is more around 10 to 30 phones per 100 people.

Programmers and data processing personnel were lost—some 50,000 of them—in the 1970s because of emigration to the United States and Israel. Information, which is both abundant and generally accurate in the West, is often vague or missing in the USSR and Eastern European nations.

The Soviet personal computer, a clone of the Apple II (the AGAT) cannot be bought, but only rented. This might be because of an attempt to control the use of the systems, which in turn might reduce a widespread enthusiasm and interest in technological progress.

Finally, attempts at producing computers closely resembling IBM-370 and DEC PDP-11s has resulted in less powerful and quite expensive machines. The use of computers is still somewhat rare, with less than 10 percent of the systems the United States has, and manual means are still the common practice in most businesses and government offices.

East Germany

East Germany, a nation that is physically closer to and has greater ties with the West, is the Eastern Bloc's largest producer of computers and the principal source of technology for the Soviet Union. In recent years East Germans have produced upward of 20,000 machines and used their own U-D processors to drive their ES and SM computers, many of which are exported to the Soviet Union.

They also build industrial robots that are used in a variety of industries, and Robotron typewriters, which are used by the Pentagon in the United States. There also is a supercomputer project underway known as MAMO, although little is known about it.

Poland

Computers are quite rare in Poland, and many computer courses are taught and run without any hands-on experience at all. Some teachers of computer science bring in photographs to show students what a computer looks like.

Because Poland cannot produce computers in sufficient quantities, importation is allowed, mostly Ataris and Commodores, and half a million have been imported already. The total count of computers for professional use numbers just around 10,000, a tiny fraction of the millions found in the West. Surprisingly, while the government does not have computers, the Polish opposition does.

Hungary

Hungary's strength is in software, and several Hungarian firms sell software for mainframes throughout the world, more than $7 million worth, mostly to the United States and Western European nations. Novotrade, a Hungarian computer firm, earned $1.5 million from sales of its 25 computer games.

Czechoslovakia, Bulgaria, and Romania

Czechoslovakia, Bulgaria, and Romania lag behind East Germany, Poland, and Hungary in many areas. Czechoslovakia does not have the funds to purchase technology; however, home systems, such as the Sinclair, are being used. Bulgaria produces magnetic disks, and is a leader in Europe in disk production. Disk drives and electronic robots are produced in Romania and exported to the Soviet Union. Romania has very few computers and is behind both in production and use.

In Summary

While Western Europe is a major competitor in the race for the fifth-generation computer, with its highly ambitious Alvey and ESPRIT programs, the Soviet Union and Eastern Europe lag behind considerably, both in research and development and in accessibility of basic computer systems. However, only the future will tell the results of the Soviet's and Eastern Europe's new programs to improve their standing in the quest for a fifth-generation computer.

Part II
Fifth-Generation Hardware and Technologies

Chapter 4
Parallel Processing

The hallmark of the computer industry has been its ability for innovation and development, characterized by its dynamic position on the cutting edge of technology. Computers grow more sophisticated, more powerful, and more flexible by orders of magnitude each year.

Advances in VLSI in microchips have caused the cost of computing on these chips to drop an average of 20 to 30 percent annually for the past three decades. At the same time, miniaturization has resulted in a roughly tenfold jump in computing speed about every seven years, an improvement by a factor of almost 10,000. Today's desktop personal computers can perform more than 50,000 floating-point operations per second, (.05 MFLOPS) while the Cray-2, one of the world's fastest computers, can do up to 1,200 MFLOPS. Computer designs already on the drawing board are projected to go over 10,000 MFLOPS. Can computing retain this momentum? Not without a radical departure from the conventional design of the computer, which has existed for almost 50 years, and its limitations.

Improvements to conventional microchips, from new methods such as x-ray lithography for chip fabrication and new materials such as gallium arsenide, can be expected to last for about another 10 to 15 years. This progress, plus the advent of new devices such as the Josephson junction and the HEMT, will make future microchips denser by a factor of 20 to 40 and probably 6 to 12 times faster than previous ones. Ultimately though, the laws of physics will inhibit further breakthroughs.

No matter how quick microprocessors become over the next 10 to 15 years, they will eventually run into the great limit of the universe: the speed of light. Nothing can travel faster. Although today's supercomputers can perform a single instruction in less than 2 nanoseconds (billionths of a second), in such a minutely tiny interval as a nanosecond, light travels only 9 inches. That means an entire instruction in a supercomputer such as this must be done within a wire path less than 18 inches long. Ironically, working at light speed begins to delay calculations as circuits simply sit idle waiting for signals to reach them from other parts of the computer.

In an attempt to minimize the distance that signals must travel, the Cray-1 design philosophy is to package components of the computer as tightly as possible, grouped together into a circle just large enough to fit a person in between. The longest wire inside the Cray-1 is 4 feet. By the Cray-2, the longest wire had been cut to 18 inches. Although the Crays experienced an incredible improvement in speed, compensating for these problems is a short-term and expensive solution. The Crays and all of the supercomputers in their class must deal with enormous power consumption and heat, and sidestepping these difficulties with coolants and low-power chips is added onto the price tag. For example, the Cray-1 sells from between $10 million and $15 million, and its cousin, the Cray-XMP, costs around $8.5 to $16 million.

Although you can obtain a microprocessor capable of doing more than 1 million instructions per second for less than $75, to get only 500 times that performance will cost you more than 200,000 times as much. Such disproportions will only widen as, on one hand, existing microchips become easier and cheaper to make, and on the other hand, it becomes prohibitive and hence more costly, to make faster chips. Computing is now at a turning point: to ensure its continuing acceleration and growth perhaps nothing less than a radical change in computers as we know them is needed. It will be necessary to start over once again.

Parallel Systems Architectures

A good analogy of modern computers today is a single worker trying to build a house alone. This worker must do the plumbing, the carpentry, the electrical wiring, and everything else one step at a time, nail by nail, in a specific order. This might seem a ridiculously slow process, but it is a good approximation of how sequential computers work: by dealing with operations one piece at a time.

A better approach might be to hire several workers to perform some of the jobs, such as bricklaying, which could be accomplished faster by more laborers working at the same time. Even better would be to split up the larger task of building the house into smaller, independent subtasks, such as plumbing and carpentry and such, and let the workers do them simultaneously in separate groups.

That is the main idea behind parallel processing. Parallel computers, or multiprocessors, will link tens, hundreds, even thousands of processors together to join their speed and harness their power to perform operations simultaneously: 1,000 computers working in concert, 10,000 times faster than a computer working alone, doing 10 billion things at once. At the moment, there is no ceiling on the sheer computing power we might be able to achieve through parallel processing. It is the second stage of the computer revolution.

Oddly enough, for a wave of the future, parallel processing is not a new idea. John von Neumann, the mathematician who laid the foundation for the serial computer architecture we use today, recognized the potential of parallel processing but put the idea aside in light of the great cost of tubes and wiring. What he designed instead, a serial, sequential machine, quickly became the standard architecture for computers and has changed little in 50 years.

ENIAC, the first general-purpose electronic computer, built in 1945 at the University of Pennsylvania to compute ballistics tables, was originally a highly parallel, decentralized machine. Computations were divided between 27 different processing units, and to solve problems, these units were interconnected to one another by hand. ENIAC's tenure as the world's first parallel computer was brief. In 1948, the separate units of the computer were reorganized in a centralized structure and reprogrammed to accept serial input, rather than parallel. ENIAC remained a serial computer for the rest of its life.

The reason for ENIAC's switch from parallel to serial processing was based on the limitations of available technology. Computer memories were only capable of storing several thousand bits of data, and this information had to be accessed one bit at a time. It was only natural for computers to deal with this in a sequential manner.

On the other hand, nature itself suggests parallelism. Look at the brain, where more than a trillion neurons, each linked to as many as a thousand others, cooperate together to perform at an astounding 10 billion operations per second. Even more amazing is the fact that the brain can think, reason, listen, and see,things that even the fastest computers today cannot do, while using circuitry a million times less complex and requiring less power than a 20-watt lightbulb. Michael L. Dertouzos, director of the MIT Lab for Computer Science, puts it succinctly: "What arrogant reasoning," he writes, "led us to believe that a single processor capable of only a few million instructions per second could ever exhibit intelligence?''

Parallel processing efforts today reflect two approaches: one aimed at improving the speed of single processors by applying parallel techniques of computation, the other at true parallelism by building systems made up of many processors linked together.

John von Neumann's original layout of the computer distinctly separates the central processing unit (CPU) from its memory. To perform an operation, the processors must first access the proper information and data required from memory; then when finished, return its output back again. A relatively slow exchange, this method forces the processor's functional units to remain idle and wasteful, no matter how speedy they are, while they wait for information to be stored to or fetched from memory.

Access to memory is complicated even further by bottlenecks of data when two or more pieces of information need to be retrieved at the same time for an operation. The reason these jams occur is that instructions have one and only one single channel to ferret data between processors and memory. This connection must deal with the flow one bit at a time, a problem that has come to be known as the von Neumann bottleneck.

Pipelining

In 1967, IBM responded to this situation by releasing the 360/91 and introducing the concept of *pipelining*. When it was introduced, the IBM 360/91 was more than twice as fast as the previous recordholder, Control Data Corporation's 6600. Upon closer inspection, the root of the von Neumann bottleneck was found to lie, not in the fact that there is only one channel to communicate with, but in the actual process of computation itself—it is inefficient. An instruction can only be executed after all the appropriate data had arrived. A relevant example of this process is to obtain all the parts for a new car, then build one. For the next car, you would assemble another set of parts, then build another, and so on. Every worker in effect, would be constructing an entire automobile alone.

The pipeline is the computing equivalent of the assembly line. The assembly line worker does not labor on a particular car individually; instead the entire job is divided into many smaller subtasks that each worker concentrates on. The benefit of the assembly line is the efficiency gained because of the large-scale repetition of tasks, which is translated into speed. The idea is not true parallel: it does not produce a thousand cars at once, but still makes them one at a time, simply faster. Pipelining works as such.

Pipelining is particularly effective for any repetitive operations. Say the instructions ask that two sets of three numbers are to be added. In machines without pipelining, an addition would take a single clock cycle, and six clock cycles to complete the additions in our example. In pipelined addition, a new pair of numbers would enter the processor every clock cycle. While this pair is operated upon, another two numbers are transferred from memory at the same time. In this way, the processor keeps things moving and can produce a sum with each clock cycle. Using pipelining, adding our two sets of three numbers would take only four cycles, not six.

Although an improvement of only 33 percent in this case might not seem spectacular, the performance receives an even greater boost when larger sets of data are involved. As with a real assembly line, pipelining is most efficient with large volumes of information. Plus, pipelines can be used to speed up all operations that require access to memory, not just computational ones, because it allows the processor to receive data on successive cycles without waiting for a complete set to arrive before accessing memory again.

Vector Processing

Often a computer must perform an identical operation on many different pieces of data. An equivalent human task is stamping envelopes. Say a person has been given 100 single stamps and puts them in the desk drawer. When this person needs to stamp an envelope, he or she must first open up the drawer, locate a stamp, get it, and then affix it to the envelope. To stamp another envelope, the whole process must be repeated. This process is analogous to how most computers deal with their data. Instead of treating every operation independently, *vector processing* organizes expressions and strings them together into long lists called *vectors*, roughly equivalent to connecting your 100 single stamps into one convenient roll. Instead of searching for a stamp in the drawer each time you want one, you merely tear off another stamp from the roll. This eliminates the need to look for data to be processed because all the values needed by the computer are already there, attached to the preceding one. The computer, using vectors, can then treat the entire list of information as one unit, and perform the whole operation on the array in a single instruction.

Although the entire task has now been reduced to just one operation, the individual elements of the vectors must still undergo repetitive calculations as before. If two vectors are to be added, the first element of one vector is added to the first element of the other, and the second elements are added together, and so on. As a result, vector processing is often coupled with pipelining in many computer architectures. The Cray-1, the first commercial vector processor, released in 1976, contained three pipelined units specifically for vector processing. These parallel techniques have allowed the Cray-1 to be more than 32 times faster than its closest competitor, the Control Data Corporation's 7600.

Almost all the supercomputers in existence today are devoted to scientific and engineering research. There they mostly are used, not for delicate technical analysis, but for the raw calculating power they contain. These superfast machines must simulate a slew of physical phenomena in such fields as aerodynamics, meteorology, and atomic physics and juggle millions of interrelated variables each second. Vector processing and pipelining are generally effective ways of increasing speed and efficiency to perform these computationally intensive problems, and have become staples within serial machines, but the key factor here is not readily available: more processing power. The methods of solving many of these time-consuming problems are well known, but for these applications, even very fast serial processors are just not good enough.

The Future of Parallel Processing

A typical task such as feature extraction (visual identification of shapes, edges, and shadows in a scene) can require more than ten thousand billion operations per second on a continuous basis in a machine. Every pixel of a picture, of which there can be more than 1 million, must be dealt with individually, measured, analyzed, and compared with others to determine edges, then joined together into shapes deduced from shading and texture. All these tasks must be performed for each pixel. These jobs lend themselves to parallel. The eye is a natural parallel processor—every pixel is attached to a single nerve fiber, allowing all the visual data to be processed simultaneously in less than a tenth of a second. A dedicated image processing computer can divide each pixel of a scene among 1 million processors in a rough analogy of the human eye.

The future of multiprocessors and parallel processing can be blocked into three crucial areas: designing computer architectures, programming them, and designing applications for them. Researchers over the past three decades have created a large number of parallel processing models varying in size, connections, and sophistication. Which is the best? There is no optimum approach as of the present, or possibly the future. The computer user will be left with the best method or machine for each particular application.

Looking at the explosion of parallel computers, the most important feature of these machines and their most crucial criteria for classification is *granularity*. Granularity is a term for the size and complexity of the processors in a system. A fine-grain multiprocessor system will generally consist of many small, relatively simple processors, somewhere between 100,000 and 10 million of them. A medium-grain system will have more powerful processors, but less of them, perhaps 10,000. At the bottom are coarse-grain systems, which have the most powerful processors, but maybe only from 2 to 100 processors in all.

Parallel processing machines exist in a variety of connection schemes, memory arrangements, and communication types. There are ring networks (FIG. 4-1A) that arrange their processors, each having two neighbors, in a circular fashion; there are mesh schemes (FIG. 4-1B), in which each node is connected to four others in a gridlike fashion. The advantage of these two designs is simplicity: although any number of processors can be connected in a ring or a mesh, the number of connections each processor must support is small (two or four respectively). Communication channels can easily handle the traffic among only a few nodes.

Perhaps the largest drawback of the ring and mesh is the number of points a message from one node to another might involve. There is no direct route between any two nodes, and communications are easily delayed by the roundabout travel. Every processor could be connected to every other processor (FIG. 4-1C), but this system would require an unwieldy number of connections. The result in the ring and mesh is that many nodes sit idle while waiting for data to arrive, and a lot of computing power is wasted.

Binary Tree Architecture

The binary tree is another simple network of connections. Starting from a single node, the binary tree doubles in size at each level; every

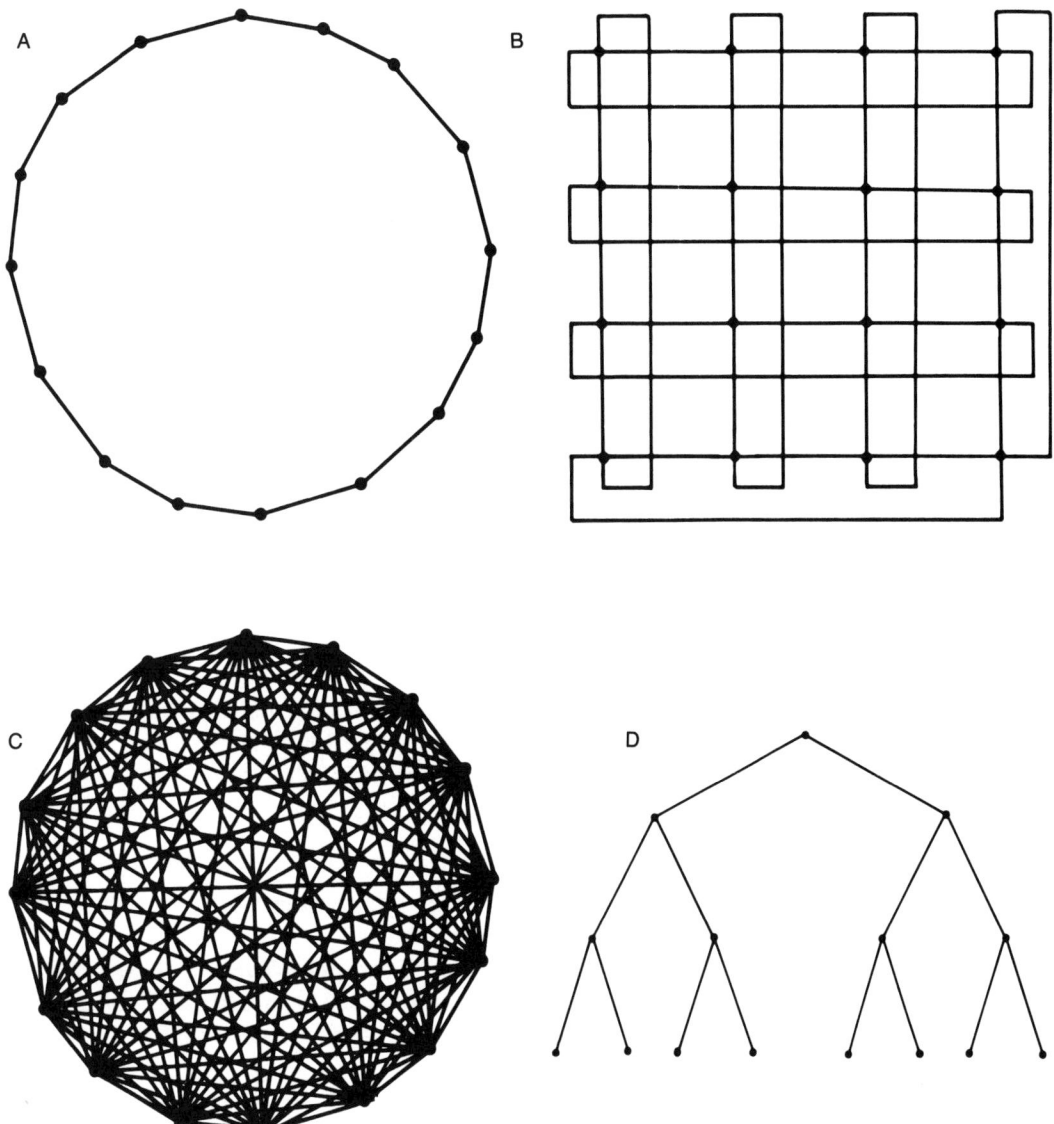

Fig. 4-1. Some major connection schemes for parallel processing. (A). Ring Network. (B). A North-South-East-West network, or "mesh" scheme. (C). An augmented ring network, where each node is connected to every other node. (D). A binary tree.

processor at every layer develops two connections branching out in different directions (FIG. 4-1D). After as few as 20 levels of branching, there are as many as 1 million "leaves" on the binary tree.

The binary tree is an exotic architecture that has little practical use. Bottlenecks form easily at branching points. Memory lies in the single "stem" node at the top; processors at the "roots" must follow lengthy path to access this memory, depending on the amount of branching in the tree. It is not surprising that the binary tree is used very little today.

Bus-based Architecture

Bus-based architecture is the most common design for multiprocessors. It is essentially an outgrowth of serial computing, a traditional serial machine with two or more CPUs. These CPUs do not have to be very simple either. For example, the Cray X-MP48 supercomputer, self-promoted as "the world's most successful parallel processor" is two or four Cray-1's tied together into a single bus-based system and attains peak speeds of more than 1,000 MIPS or more in 100 percent vectorizable situations, although it rarely does.

The main advantage of bus-based computing is compatibility and ease of operation. By using proven technology, bus-based systems can take advantage of the many years of experience behind them. Software only needs to be modified, instead of overhauled, to fit a strange new hardware logic. Also, the short-term cost is relatively cheap in comparison with the expense of creating a new hardware architecture from scratch.

Bus based computers work with a global memory that processors can reach via a central communication channel. This memory serves as a common ground where any processor can leave information for others to subsequently read or vice versa. However, this "computing by committee" can result in communications overload when the amount of processors manipulating this memory surpasses capacity. Periods of peak activity can produce very long delays.

To combat this bottleneck, bus-based systems generally contain small amounts of processors—around 20—and use tight wiring and close interconnections. It is often a very difficult and expensive order, but yet much easier than engineering an entirely different architecture.

Bus-based computers are true multiprocessors only in the widest sense. Programs are broken into several pieces that are distributed along with data to the individual processors, where they more or less run independently of one another unless information must be exchanged. This operation is called *multiple-instruction-stream/multiple-data-stream*. Each processor in a bus-based system is in actuality an independent computer; they are just synchronized and coordinated together to work as a unit.

The biggest drawback of shared-memory, bus-based machines is the memory itself. Fighting congestion and bottlenecking in order to keep access at an optimum is difficult and is not cheap. If the different processors must battle among themselves for memory access, why not just supply each one of them with some memory of their own? This scheme is called *distributed-memory architecture*.

Distributed memory is often also called *single-instruction/multiple-data* (SIMD) processing. The data all the processors operate on can differ widely as the words *multiple-data* suggest, but they will all follow one or a few commands. A good example of SIMD processing is a baseball stadium, filled with people sitting in their chairs holding numbered tickets. Over the loudspeaker, a voice tells them all to look at their tickets and stand up if their ticket number is odd. Simultaneously, 50,000 people look at their tickets and do the appropriate action. SIMD processing is ideally tailored for similar, repetitive calculations on large amounts of data.

In a distributed-memory machine, data is sent at the beginning of the computation to all the processors involved. Every processor will be able to concentrate on its particular piece of data received. During the course of the computation however, many processors will need to share data with others, or receive additional inputs. The keys to an efficient, rapid distributed-memory computer are several: to attain the quickest, shortest connections for communications between any nodes; to minimize the amount of interpathways necessary; and to match the right scheme of distributed memory to the application at hand.

N-Dimensional Cube Architecture

The *hypercube*, or *n*-cube, architecture can be dubbed the "nemesis" of the bus-based machines. Whatever advantages bus-based systems have from compatibility and ease of use are offset by the computing power and potential of the hypercube.

In brief, a hypercube is a multidimensional shape of *n* dimensions, hence its other name *n*-cube. At the least, a cube that had zero dimensions would be a point (see FIG. 4-2). To create its one-dimensional ana-

50 Parallel Processing

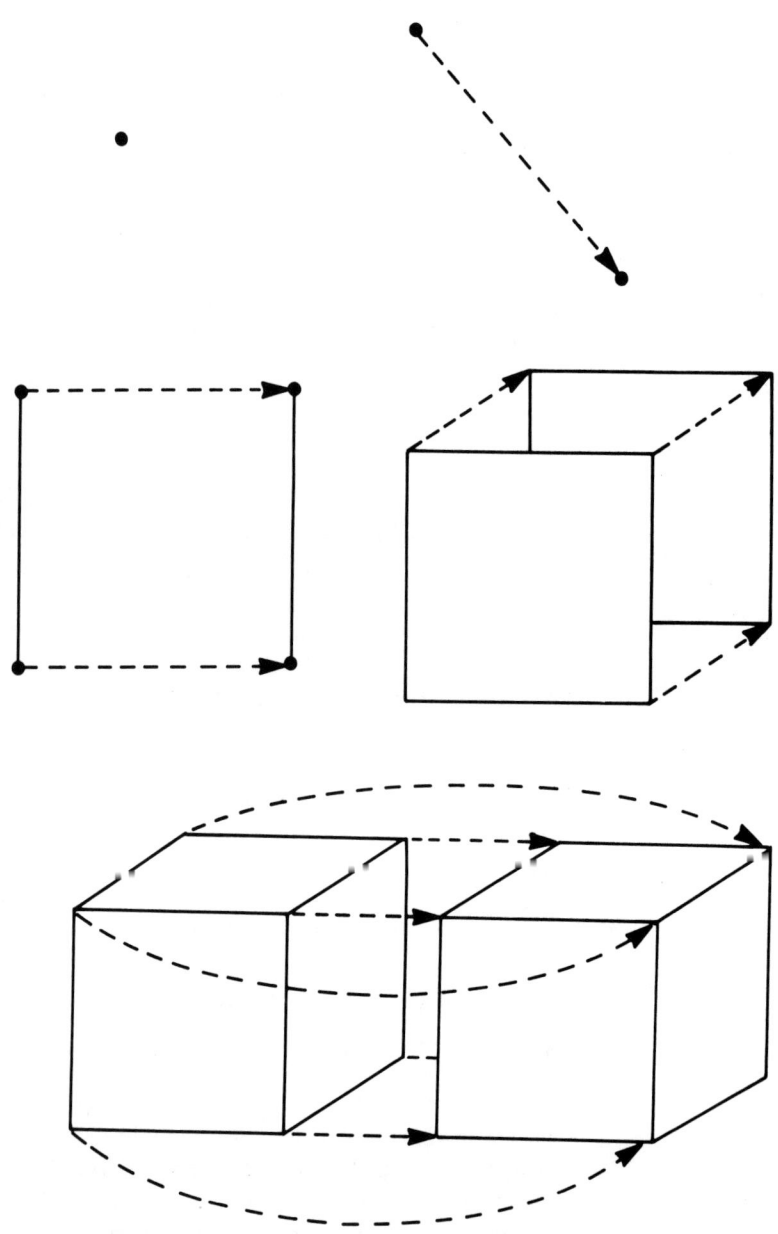

Fig. 4-2. Various dimensional "hypercubes." Starting with a one-dimensional hypercube, which is a point, and moving from left to right, are different dimensional stages: a line, a square, a cube, and finally, a four-dimensional hypercube. The Connection Machine's hypercube, for example, is six-dimensional.

log, a straight line, imagine two connected points. For example to create a two-dimensional figure, take two straight lines and connect them together to form a square. Now imagine a processor at each vertex of the multidimensional cube, such as the four corners on a square, and communications running between lines connecting the corners. In general, an n-dimensional cube will have 2^n nodes.

Although we live in three dimensions, it is possible to construct a four-dimensional hypercube by using two three-dimensional hypercubes and juxtaposing them so that each vertex of each cube is attached to the corresponding vertex on the other. The result is not only twice as many processors, but also a more efficient way of connecting many devices together. In a four-dimensional hypercube, the longest path connecting any two nodes is four communication lines. The unique structure of a hypercube precludes the need to wire every single processor to every other and still ensures an efficient data path. In an n-dimensional hypercube, the longest path is n.

Hypercubes up to almost any dimension desired can be fabricated simply by geometric manipulations. A 16-dimensional hypercube consisting of 65,536 processors is the practical limit of these machines currently. An attempt to connect 65,536 processors together by wiring each one to the 65,535 others would take over 2 billion wires. Other hypercubes on the drawing board are projected to have 256,000 processors and up.

It is only in sheer numbers that one can experience the true potential of the hypercube. But to remain flexible to the needs of their buyers, computer companies offer broad varieties of cube configurations, ranging from 4 to 65,536 processors, which are able to reach theoretical peak speeds of over 262 billion floating-point operations per second (GFLOPS).

There is no coincidence that the hypercube class of computers is dominated by fine-grain machines. This fact is treated by some critics as the hypercube's largest weakness, and many still remain unconvinced in the hypercube's ability to perform outside of very narrow, vertical applications such as image processing or modeling physical phenomena. But hypercubes have not yet had their expansion capabilities exploited fully and have not even approached that level of development. Instead, now hypercubes are a rather conservative, relatively inexpensive approach that seems to have the most potential over time.

Dataflow Architecture

Traditional serial computers are limited to following a list of instructions, step by step. Parallel computers (FIGS. 4-3 and 4-4) free researchers to experiment, innovate, and imagine radically different approaches to programming and control. One of these new computing strategies is the concept of *dataflow*, pioneered by Jack Dennis at MIT. In a simple view, the "flow" of program logic in a dataflow machine is determined by the data used in the operation itself. Data is sent to and from a processor as it is needed or completed. A properly running dataflow machine should be able to maintain a constant stream of information moving toward the solution.

The organization of a dataflow machine is roughly reminiscent of a railroad switch yard. All the processors, usually less than 100 because of the coarse-grained nature of most dataflow machines, are connected centrally to this switch yard. Before beginning a computation, instructions for each processor are distributed among them. Once the calculations start, the processors begin to produce results. This new data is *tagged*, or marked with the information of where it should go and how it should be used. The central switch yard will be able to read these "tags" and determine their appropriate routes.

A particular node in a dataflow machine (FIG. 4-5) cannot operate until all the necessary data arrive, and must wait for them before proceeding onto their next step like some electronic relay race. Unused nodes are left to sit idle. But by waiting for the required data, the dataflow machine eliminates the danger of clashing with the ongoing work of other processors and creating a bottleneck. When the waited for operands come, they are acted upon, tagged, and sent back into the network again. The advantage of dataflow is that the user merely needs to specify instructions to be completed and allocate the right information to the processors once, and then let the flow of data reach a solution itself without having to be burdened with exact steps, procedures, or details of the execution.

As the dataflow network grows, it has difficulty in dealing with its increased size and complexity. There are more communications, wiring, processors, and expenses. Eventually, the cost becomes impractical and prohibitive to continue, which is the reason why most dataflow machines are coarse grained. But if dataflow is to become an effective alternative, it must be able to cope with the tremendously large databases of real-world applications and artificial intelligence.

Fig. 4-3. The NCUBE/seven parallel processing system. A compact (desk height and 15 inches wide) multiuser system, it is a good representative example of a parallel processing computer, supporting 128 processing nodes for performance at around 250 MIPS. It exemplifies the trend toward more powerful computing in the office environment, instead of the lab. (photo courtesy NCUBE Corporation, Beaverton, Oregon)

Fig. 4-4. An NCUBE host board (photo courtesy NCUBE Corporation, Beaverton, Oregon)

Parallel Systems Programming

A number of obstacles lie in front of parallel processing's successful push forward into the technological arena. First of all is the lack or limited availability of programming or programs on parallel machines. So far, little progress has been made in the task of telling these parallel machines what to do. A whole new family of languages will have to be created for multiprocessor applications, and that will require a lot of effort because of the sheer coordination these new languages must have. Software almost always lags behind hardware, and this might prove detrimental to parallel processing. Although some researchers might build a machine made up of 1 million processors that can theoretically go faster than anything on earth, it might all prove naught if the soft-

Fig. 4-5. *A parallel computing node consisting of just seven chips: a VLSI processor and six memory chips. The processing nodes are interconnected in a hypercube using the integrated communication links, and can be mapped onto nearly any useful topology, including rings, grids, and trees. A typical processor board consists of 64 nodes interconnected in an order six hypercube, with one or more boards plugged together to make a system. (photo courtesy NCUBE Corporation, Beaverton, Oregon)*

ware to run it does not exist. The level of performance is directly related to the level of the software involved. Major progress is needed and a significant effort must be made to restructure programming or rewrite basic applications for these new machines.

Another problem that parallel machines will face is the possibility of increased errors and malfunctions in both hardware and software. A serial processor might have an error rate of one per few thousand hours. Imagine the error rate of a 1,000-processor system. Hardware failures might occur hourly, and the system is limited to being functional only a small fraction of the time. Computer reliability is a pressing and all-important issue for an effective parallel processing computer.

One final drawback, although perhaps minor, of the current crop of parallel processing machines is the lack of standard benchmarks to evaluate and compare performance between the wide variety of the field. Because separating parallel architectures into specific classes is so difficult, the best way to determine how suitable a particular model is for a certain application is to run it through a set of representative benchmarks. Perhaps through trial-and-error some optimum system can be found. Benchmarks might be the perfect way to introduce some standards into a market that has so far ignored them. The National Bureau of Standards has been working on parallel-computing benchmarks, and has begun distributing them through Arpanet, the Defense communications network. Industry has yet to play an active role in encouraging further standardization to provide a stable foundation for development to come.

Despite any limiting factors on the side, the outlook for parallel processing is still sunny. Current parallel processing hardware and software is rudimentary, primitive, and in a relative state of infancy. No doubt technology will improve in the future. New semiconductors, new designs, and new methods of communication, such as optical interconnects, will help parallel processing grow and mature. Potential is parallel processing's biggest advantage. There are no limits to the possibilities, and one can optimistically note that we are only at the beginning.

Chapter 5
Microchips and Microchip Technologies

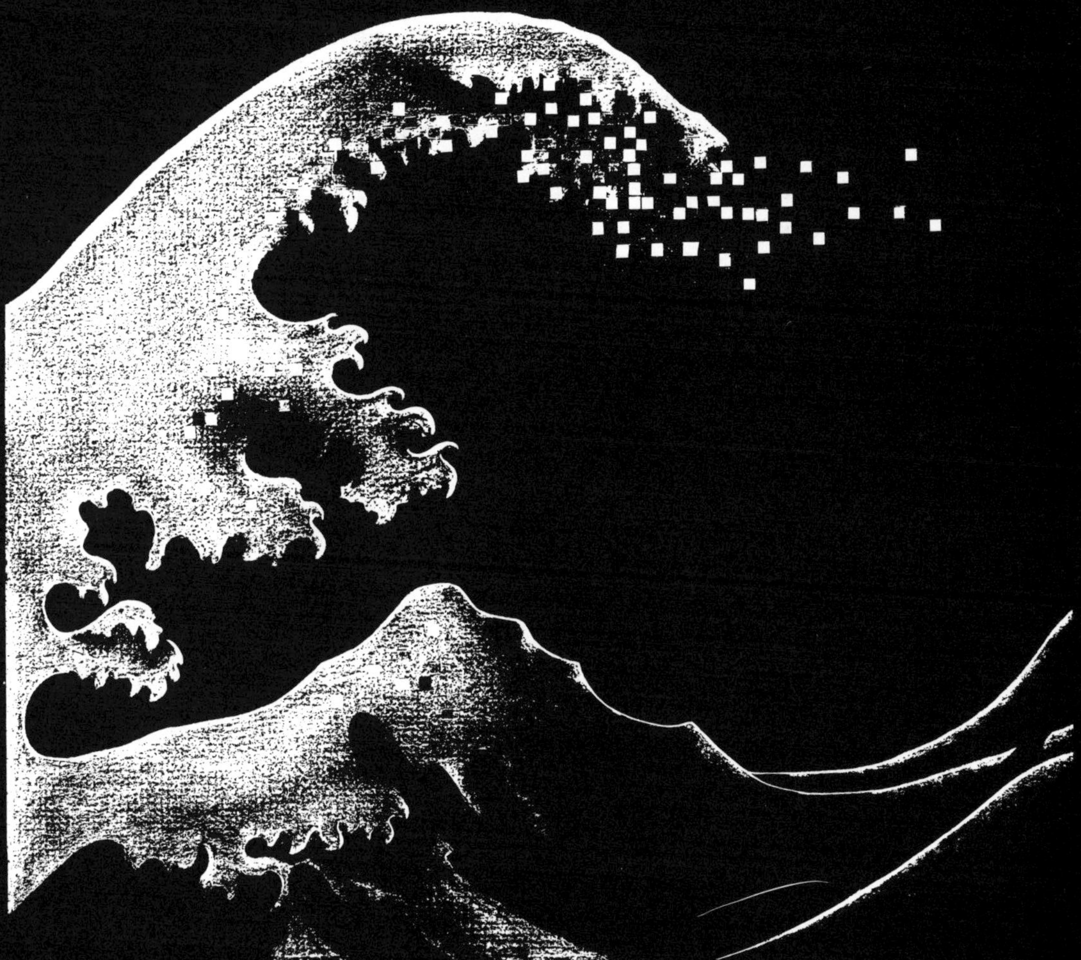

In its very short history, computer technology has come a long way from the early computing behemoths that filled entire rooms with their bulk and noise. These computers were slow, and could perform only a few thousand arithmetic operations a second, about as fast as some present day calculators. In contrast, today's computer is an efficient machine of blinding speed, and can perform more than 10 billion operations per second, almost 10 million times faster than those early machines. If the aviation industry had developed at the rate computer technology has over the last half century, a jet airliner today would cost only $500, and would be able to circumnavigate the globe in 20 minutes on only 5 gallons of gasoline. A computer that would have been as large as a football field 40 years ago has been reduced to a single chip 100,000 times faster at one one-hundredth of the cost.

But what next? What is the future of computer technology? Tomorrow's computers will contain more power and more speed in less space than ever before. They will be intelligent and easier to use and operate. They will be a million times more powerful than anything in existence today, and in a package a hundred times smaller. They will have the ability to converse in spoken English, manipulate ideas and concepts, learn and associate from experience, make decisions, and perform tasks just like any human being.

Researchers all over the world are working hard to turn that vision into reality, and are exploring a variety of promising new technologies and materials. These technologies and materials include gallium arsenide, an advanced semiconductor material for superfast computer chips; new semiconductor chip techniques that pack more transistors onto a single chip; and high-speed semiconductor transistors, such as the HEMT and the Ballistic Transistor. Exotic new ideas include the transphasor and the SEED, which run on light instead of electricity.

Josephson junctions, which must be kept at supercold temperatures—around −270 degrees Fahrenheit—in order to operate; and molecular transistors made out of organic molecules, so small that 200,000 of these transistors would be able to fit across the width of a period. Although some of these ideas border on the fantastic, they are all a part of what is to come in the fifth generation.

Semiconductor Technologies

Since the invention of the transistor in 1947, semiconductors have dominated the electronics industry. More than 40 years of experience with semiconductors have made them into a staple of the electronics world. Today microchips form the heart of practically every electronic device in use, from computer chips to solar cells. They are responsible for everything from supercomputers to digital watches and electronic coffee machines. Semiconductors have revolutionized the world, and are undergoing a revolution themselves. It is predicted that by as early as the mid-1990s the computing power of a dozen of today's supercomputers will fit on a single integrated circuit.

Indeed, the sophisticated applications of semiconductors today represent only a fraction of what will be possible in the near future. These superchips will not only make personal robots a reality, but will allow computerized car engines with lower emissions, higher mileage, and better performance. Superchips will be inside digital televisions with superior quality broadcasts, resolution, and sound. "Smart" computers powered with superchips will understand speech, "see," and make complicated human decisions. Perhaps the greatest application of these superchips might be in the Strategic Defense Initiative (SDI), where such "smart" computers would be essential to maintain the complex defenses required. This is one additional reason why the government is such a major supporter of semiconductor research.

Semiconductors dominate electronics today. Their extreme versatility and the great advances that have been made with them will probably allow semiconductors to continue dominating in the future.

Silicon is the reigning "king" of semiconductor materials. Abundant and easy to work with, silicon has been used for more than 40 years. As a semiconductor, silicon acts as both a good conductor and a good insulator of electricity. But silicon in its pure state does not conduct electricity at all. To make silicon into a semiconductor, silicon is "doped"

Fig. 5-1. A typical VLSI processor. The single chip integrates a general purpose 32 bit processor (including high speed 32 and 64 bit floating point), an error correcting memory interface and 22 independent direct memory access communication links. A parallel processing computer can use as many as 1024 of these processors connected in tandem to achieve high-performance speeds (up to 2000 MIPS) at relatively low-cost. (photo courtesy NCUBE Corporation, Beaverton, Oregon)

with an impurity. This means that an element is added to silicon to give it semiconductor properties. Once added, the "doped" silicon becomes a conductor, but retains some of its original nonconducting properties. Thus silicon becomes a semiconductor (FIG. 5-1).

The HEMT

Inside conventional silicon transistors, electrons must flow through the semiconductor material for the device to operate. These electrons traveling through silicon must cope with the defects and impurities "doped" inside, which act as obstacles in their path (FIG. 5-2A). The High-Electron-Mobility-Transistor (HEMT) overcomes this problem,

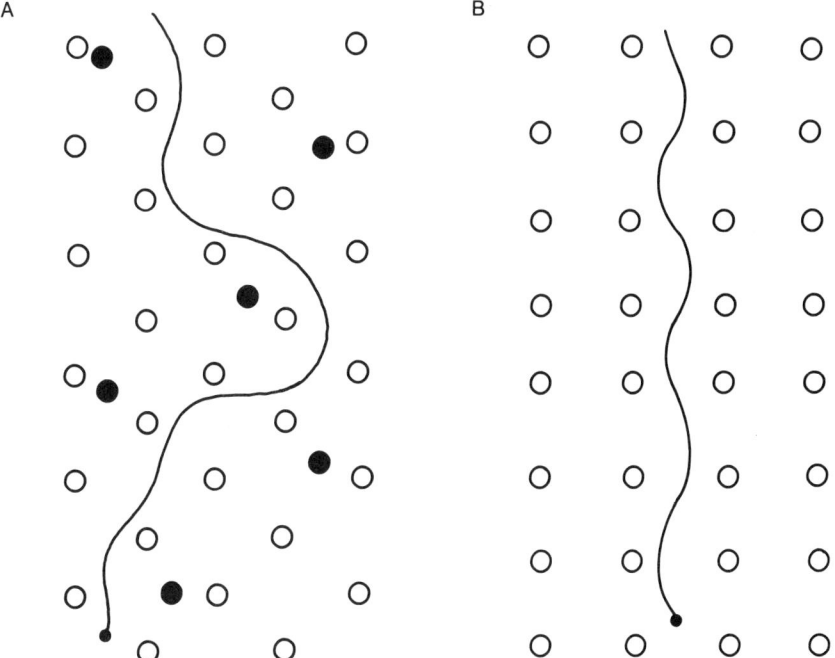

Fig. 5-2. *Electron movement within the transistor. In conventional transistors, such as the one depicted in A, the electron's path is a roundabout journey through obstacles and irregularities in the material's structure. Ballistic transistors, such as the one depicted in B, will allow electrons to pass with relatively little interference, translating into faster transistor switching speeds.*

"channeling" electrons into paths containing less of these impurities. These electrons, no longer hampered by obstacles in their way, are able to travel much more quickly and allow the HEMT to achieve extraordinary speeds (FIG. 5-2B.)

Although basically very similar to a conventional transistor, the HEMT is made up of *heterostructures*, or very thin, multilayered sandwiches of compounds such as gallium arsenide and gallium aluminum arsenide. These two compounds are alternately layered throughout the heterostructure. When electrons flow through the heterostructure, they are channeled toward the gallium arsenide layers. Gallium arsenide is the pure form of gallium aluminum arsenide and contains few defects or impurities; it is relatively "perfect." Electrons that are channeled into the gallium arsenide layers encounter less impurities and defects, and thus achieve greater speeds. Indeed, electron speeds in the HEMT are more than three times faster than conventional semiconductors. At such speeds, HEMTs have been slated to play an important role in the supercomputers of tomorrow. The Japanese Superspeed Project and the United States' Strategic Computing Initiative are both concentrating their efforts on the HEMT and other related technologies.

Ballistic Transistors

Another semiconductor technology is the ballistic transistor. Electrons inside a ballistic transistor travel through very thin layers of material and encounter very little resistance against their motion. Unhindered by opposition, these electrons achieve numbing speeds unparalleled by conventional technology today, and allow electrons to travel like projectiles inside the ballistic transistor.

The key to making ballistic transistors is to make the layers the electrons travel through very thin layers of material. The layer of material an electron must travel through inside conventional transistors is comparable to a large crowd of people. Any person wishing to pass through a large crowd would be slowed down considerably. Electrons inside conventional transistors are slowed by the material they must travel through. Inside the ballistic transistor, the layers of material would be comparable to a long line of people standing single file. It is very easy to cut across this line and any person wishing to pass through will not encounter much resistance. The layers of material inside the ballistic transistor would be extremely thin—100 times thinner than the semiconductor layers currently in use today.

Already, researchers at IBM have constructed ballistic transistor layers made of gallium arsenide only 300 angstroms thick (One angstrom being one ten-millionth of a meter), sandwiched between two layers of gallium aluminum arsenide into a small heterostructure. The results are dramatic. More than half of the electrons in the experimental ballistic transistor were able to travel unimpeded through the thin film. IBM is hardly alone in its work. Also, researchers at Bell Labs, Cornell University, the University of Illinois, and other institutions are busy working on ballistic transistor projects. If successful, ballistic transistors might achieve switching speeds hundreds, possibly thousands, of times faster than transistors today.

Photolithography

While speedier transistors are one objective of the fifth generation, making them smaller is another. As their size decreases, the overall speed of the microchip improves as a result of the smaller distances impulses must travel. Consequently, the key to microchip speed lies in making denser and denser chips. Researchers can pack more than 1,000,000 transistors onto a single piece of silicon only one centimeter square, transforming it into a complex network of components and metallic "highways."

To create these elaborate designs, chip makers use a technique called *photolithography*. In photolithography, a chip pattern is reduced using a series of lenses and is exposed onto the surface of the microchip, much like a telescope. This way, the miniscule details on a microchip can be worked out on a larger scale and then reduced to their proper size. Before it is exposed to the pattern, the chip is coated with a very thin layer of light-sensitive photoresist, a material that hardens upon exposure to light. When the pattern is exposed onto the chip, the photoresist hardens into a negative image of the design. This hardened, exposed photoresist is then washed away, and these tiny areas are covered, etched, and filled with semiconductor material. This material forms the tiny components and wires of the chip. After all the semiconductor material has been deposited, the remaining photoresist is washed off, leaving the microchip and its complex circuitry behind.

As photolithography improves, chipmakers are finding it more and more difficult to squeeze out even small gains in chip densities, limited by the physical capabilities of their equipment. One new photolithography technique promises to drive these chip densities even higher. In this process, called *stepping*, an enlarged portion of the chip pattern is exposed in steps, or parts, onto the surface of the microchip. After each portion is projected onto the chip, the exposure is mechanically stepped to a new site. This process is repeated until the entire microchip is exposed. The stepping process can produce circuit lines as small as .5 microns (1 micron is one-millionth of a meter), twice as small as conventional circuit lines. In comparison, a strand of hair is over 100 microns wide.

Another way to improve chip densities is to use a finer wavelength of light. Currently, ultraviolet light is used in photolithography. Although ultraviolet light's wavelength is relatively fine, the even smaller wavelength of x-rays could be used to create much thinner circuit lines, perhaps only .1 microns wide. Not only are x-rays a much finer light source, but x-rays can pass directly through the dust and particles that hamper current ultraviolet projectors and still retain a large depth of focus, which is important for clear resolution on the chip. In addition, x-rays are very low energy beams, which minimizes the scattering effects of the photoresist and provides more accurate reproductions of the chip pattern. There have been many design problems with x-rays, which keep it from active competition with current ultraviolet lithography systems.

Electron beams have been considered for photolithography as an alternative to ultraviolet light or x-rays. Unlike x-rays, electron-beam technology has built up a tremendous backlog of design and operational experience, and is looked upon as a good candidate for photolithography because of the very fine nature of electron beams. Electron beams could write chip patterns directly onto the photoresist, without requiring any expensive and time-consuming lenses or projection apparatus. This not only streamlines the rather complex process of photolithography, but also reduces the chance of any error or defects. Line resolutions of less than .5 microns have already been achieved using electron beams.

The high cost of electron beam machines has limited their widespread use. An electron beam machine can run up to $3 million or $4 million, as compared to around $750,000 for a conventional optical system. In addition, electron-beam machines are very slow and are unsuitable for high volume chip production. But according to projections, electron beams are on the rise, and promise to replace optical lithography within a decade.

Wafer-Scale Integration

In a different approach to chip density, wafer-scale integration does not attempt to improve the concentration of the components on a chip, but the concentration of the chips themselves. In wafer-scale integration, researchers can pack as many as 100 chips onto a single wafer of silicon 4 inches in diameter. The greater circuit densities achieved from this *superwafer* allow for faster computer architectures and eliminate miles of wiring, which are a frequent source of malfunction. An entire computer can be reduced to a single wafer, devoid of bulky components. Signals traveling inside this superwafer travel much more quickly because of the shorter distances between chips. However, several problems stand in the way of wafer-scale integration that must first be solved.

Ordinarily, the number of defects that arise in chip production increase in proportion to the size of the chips being built. In wafer-scale integration, as the chips being produced approach wafer size, researchers must cope with defects rates of 50 percent. In conventional microchip fabrication, defective chips simply can be discarded. The high manufacturing costs of wafer-scale integration would make this impractical and costly.

One solution to this problem is being pioneered by Mosaic Systems of Troy, Michigan. Mosaic Systems has devised a hybrid approach to wafer-scale integration. The company's founder and president, Robert Johnson, began this method in 1979 at the Burroughs Corporation. He left Burroughs in 1982 to start Mosaic Systems with $10 million in venture capital. Mosaic Systems avoids direct fabrication of the wafers, and instead buys pretested chips for use that are then attached onto the wafer. The wafer is prepared with two fine wire grids, creating more than 1.5 million intersections of wiring, each intersection separated from the next by a thin barrier of nonconductive silicon. Once all the defective lines within the wafer are determined, a computer is used to find the most efficient wiring paths to connect the chips on the wafer. Once these wiring paths are computed, an electrical impulse is simply sent through the paths, transforming the previously nonconductive silicon into a conductor, forming the wiring of the wafer and bypassing all the defective portions.

As chips reach the densities of wafer-scale integration, immense heat begins to build up among the chips. (A single wafer might create more than 1,000 watts of heat.) To operate and prevent the heat from destroying the chips, cooling systems using helium gas are used to draw away heat, or, alternately, the wafer is submerged inside liquid nitrogen at temperatures hovering above absolute zero, or −270 degrees Fahrenheit.

This tremendous circuit density not only leads to a large amount of heat, but also to electromigration, the extraneous movement of signals and material from one circuit to another. The circuit lines in wafer-scale integration are placed so closely together that material from one line can actually move to another. This can result in false signals and noise as errant signals are triggered, or can even lead to the depletion of material from one portion of the wafer as materials migrate to other portions of the chip, resulting in chip failure or short circuits.

Until now, most commercial efforts at wafer-scale integration have come up with little success. IBM, Toshiba, Texas Instruments, and a host of other companies all have been unable to produce wafer-scale integration economically. But the lure of wafer-scale integration and smaller, faster, cheaper computers still remains.

Gallium Arsenide

While researchers work on faster transistors and smaller microchips, the search for computer speed has led some researchers to faster materials as well. Silicon, the familiar workhorse of electronics, is now being confronted with an even better, more versatile material: gallium arsenide. For the last 25 years, gallium arsenide has been used for signal processing with satellites, radio, microwaves, and other related areas. But now gallium arsenide is poised for a quantum leap into a revolution in electronics.

Gallium arsenide's greatest advantage over silicon is its speed. It moves electrons 3 to 9 times faster than silicon, and gallium arsenide transistors are projected to be up to 50 times faster than conventional silicon ones. Not only will gallium arsenide make supercomputers with tremendous power possible, but it will make possible smaller cellular car phones, collision warning systems for cars, smarter robots, better medical instruments, and portable terminals linked by satellite.

The reasons for gallium arsenide's speed lie in its atomic structure. Electrons inside gallium arsenide are able to move very quickly because of the unique energy levels of gallium arsenide's atomic structure. These energy levels give electrons inside gallium arsenide more freedom of movement and allow electrons to move more rapidly through the material.

In addition to its speed, gallium arsenide has a host of other unique traits. Its optoelectronic properties allowed it to quickly grab most of the $500 million-a-year optoelectronics market because gallium arsenide can emit light, something even silicon cannot do. Gallium arsenide has been used to make solid-state lasers and light-emitting diodes as small as a grain of salt. These tiny lasers have found their way into compact disk players and fiberoptic lines, and light-emitting diodes are widely used for computer, instrument, and VCR displays, bringing up the possibility of gallium arsenide lasers and other optoelectronic devices.

Gallium arsenide also is more resistant to radiation than silicon, an important property for space satellite applications, which are exposed to damaging levels of radiation. Gallium arsenide is able to sustain radiation dosages 10,000 times silicon's radiation limit. In addition, gallium arsenide can operate with less power and in higher temperatures than silicon can, over a span of temperatures ranging from −200 to +200 degrees Celsius. As a result, gallium arsenide chips can operate under large amounts of heat, unlike more fragile silicon chips.

Silicon is not the best semiconductor material, but its great abundance and ease of use as a material have allowed it to dominate the electronics world for 40 years. In contrast to silicon's great abundance, gallium is a very rare element, making up less than .01 percent of the earth's crust. Pure gallium arsenide is difficult to obtain because of the many impurities that arise during fabrication. The rarity of gallium metal and the difficulties of its production has kept gallium arsenide in short supply at correspondingly high prices. A single 3-inch wafer of gallium arsenide can cost $250, while a 6-inch wafer of silicon can cost about $30. But new breakthroughs are changing all that. Although gallium arsenide chips have been available since 1984, gallium arsenide technology lags over a decade behind silicon. At present, gallium arsenide chips might contain a few tens of thousands of components at best, as opposed to silicon chips, which might have more than a million. But new innovations in gallium arsenide fabrication have produced improvements in its quality and its chip density. Many analysts believe gallium arsenide is on the verge of becoming a billion dollar industry by 1990.

The future of this powerful material has lured a host of companies to enter the gallium arsenide race. The gallium arsenide portion of the semiconductor industry alone is expected to make up more than one-third of the industry's business by the end of the century, amounting to $50 billion annually. Many of the biggest names in electronics, including Motorola, IBM, RCA, Texas Instruments, NEC, and Fujitsu have all begun furious research and production of gallium arsenide. Gallium arsenide even has its own answer to the Silicon Valley: Gallium Gulch, a small nucleus of start-up companies devoted to gallium arsenide production, among them Pivot III-V, Anadigics, Lytel, and AT&T's Bell labs. Other companies joining the gallium arsenide bandwagon include GigaBit Logic, the first venture capital company set up expressly for gallium arsenide, Vitesse Electronics, Rockwell International, Tektronix, and Ford. The companies will lead the way for many others to bring gallium arsenide into widespread use.

Optical Technologies

Light might be the key to the future of computing. After all, "What travels faster than light?" By definition, light's speed is a constant 186,000 miles per second, and researchers around the world are hoping to harness that blazing speed. Optical computers are not a new idea, and major advances in optical technology have been pouring from research labs worldwide, ranging from GTE, Xerox, and The Tokyo Institute of Technology to Scotland's Heriot-Watt University and AT&T's Bell Labs. Recent breakthroughs might make a full-fledged optical computer prototype a reality by as early as 1990. If so, it would herald a new era for computer technology.

Optical computers promise speeds thousands—even millions—of times faster than even the fastest supercomputers of today. While silicon transistors are theorized to have a projected speed limit of 50 picoseconds, or trillionths of a second, optical transistors might reach speeds as fast as 1 femtosecond, or quadrillionth of a second (a million-billionths of a second).

With such fantastic speeds at their disposal, optical computers will open the doors to a variety of new possibilities from engineering advanced aircraft to simulating them. An optical computer the size of a briefcase would be able to pack the raw computing power of 2,000 of today's fastest supercomputers. These computers would be able to crack unbreakable codes and simulate a nuclear explosion. Optical computers also might form the cornerstone of SDI. Indeed, the Defense Department and SDI are major proponents of optical computing research, which is projected to require up to $100 million in funding in order to develop.

But the Defense Department is not alone in its effort. The Optical Circuit Cooperative, a consortium formed three years ago at the University of Arizona of a dozen companies including Boeing, IBM, DuPont and TRW, is busy working on its own effort. Europe has already set up an optical computing project involving scientists from West Germany, Italy, France, Britain, and Belgium. Also, Japan's electronics giants, such as NEC, Matsushita, Hitachi, and Fujitsu, have put together a cooperative 10-year effort with funding from the Japanese government.

If successful, optical computer chips will have several distinct advantages over silicon. Light will not interfere with itself like electrons do, and so optical computer chips might be able to process multiple signals simultaneously—millions at a time—without losing the identity of any signal, and without fearing that the signals might interfere with each other. In contrast, conventional microchips only process one signal at a time to avoid interference. A single optical chip might be able to handle 10 billion signals per second, 10 times the capacity of today's supercomputers. This multiple processing capability might be exactly what is required for parallel processing—a computing method that allows computers to work on problems by processing multiple streams of data simultaneously, in a manner much like the human brain. Parallel processing would open the door to true artificial intelligence and allow computers to see, talk, and reason more effectively.

Another major advantage of optical computing is that it would work on analog, as opposed to digital, principles. Conventional silicon chips are digital, and work by manipulating the binary numbers 1 and 0 with strict logical accuracy. But optical computers will not be limited by the hard logic of 1's and 0's. Light is very much like a wave, curving up and down in crests and troughs. The top of the wave, its crest, can be considered as one state. The bottom of the wave, the trough, can be considered as another. The sloping area between these two parts of the wave can be broken up into an infinite amount of parts. If each of these parts is considered as another state, light can contain an unlimited number of states, as opposed to the digital 1 and 0 conventional silicon is limited to.

Not only will analog optical chips be able to choose from an infinite amount of states, but analog states can be altered far more rapidly than any digital computer can manipulate billions of ones and zeroes. In addition, these infinite states can be used to represent symbols: ideas, images, and concepts, a sheer breakaway from the rigid logic of ones and zeroes. Imagine a word processor on an optical computer that understands words and has generalized concepts of what they mean, manipulating words as easily as any human being. Right now, the only true symbolic processing is done inside the brain.

The first priority for an optical computer is a device to manipulate light, somewhat like a switch. This transistor equivalent would be the basis for the optical computer of tomorrow. Already, researchers are exploring several different possibilities for this *optical transistor*.

The Transphasor

One of the possibilities for the optical transistor is the transphasor. Pioneered by researchers at Heriot-Watt University in Edinburgh, Scotland, their transistor-like device, called the transphasor, is a small, cryogenically cooled rectangular crystal made of indium antimonide, a semiconductor. When a single light impulse is directed at the device, it is simply absorbed by the crystal (FIG. 5-3A). This is the transphasor's "off" state. When a second weaker beam is combined with the first, the first impulse bursts out of the crystal and continues traveling (FIG. 5-3B). This is the transphasor's "on" state. These two states are analogous to the two states of a conventional transistor.

The transphasor works on the principle of the Fabry-Perot interferometer, a device invented by French physicists Charles Fabry and Alfred Perot in 1896 to measure wavelengths of light. The interferometer is simply two mirrors facing each other. When light strikes one of

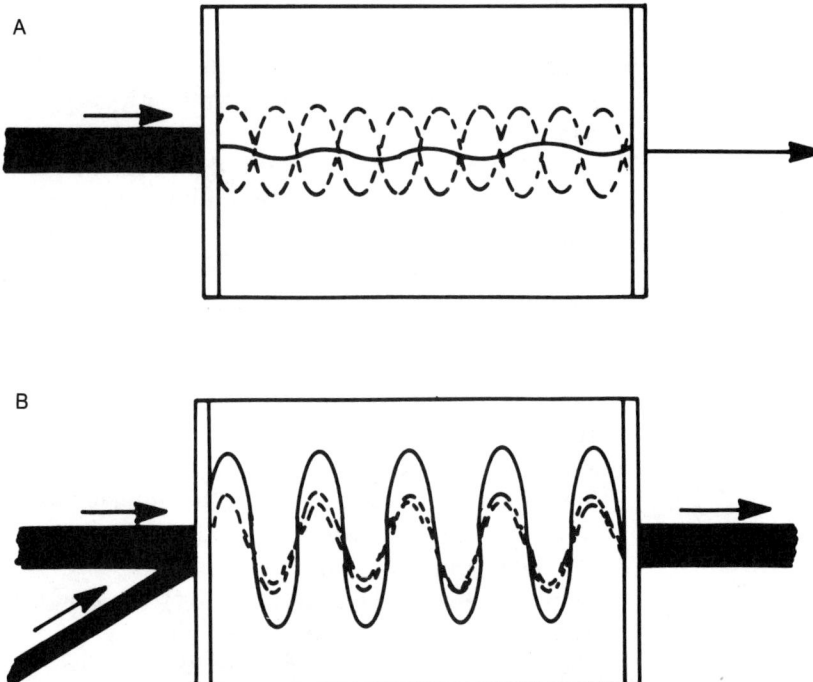

Fig. 5-3. An "optical" transistor. A constant beam of light entering the transistor (A) will be reflected back and forth between the two mirrored sides of the device, weakening it, and the output signal transmitted from the opposite end will be negligible. Upon the introduction of a second incident beam (B) the two sets of light waves will combine and reinforce each other, producing an output signal that is comparably equal to the original. The ability to toggle between these two states, a weak output and a strong one, makes the optical transistor analogous to more conventional devices.

the mirrors, the light bounces back and forth between the two mirrors infinitely.

Inside the transphasor, the two opposite ends of the crystal are mirrored inward, and act like two mirrors in a Fabry-Perot interferometer. These two mirrored ends of the crystal are partially reflecting, meaning that they reflect only a fraction of the light striking them. When a light impulse enters the transphasor and strikes one of the mirrors, only a fraction of its strength is reflected back. As the impulse bounces back and forth between the two mirrors inside the crystal, it gradually loses strength and disappears. When the light impulse is absorbed by the transphasor in this manner, it is considered "off."

When a second, weaker beam is projected into the transphasor, increasing the intensity of the first slightly, a major threshold is reached and the two beams align together and begin to amplify and reinforce each other, causing the resulting beam to suddenly gather enough strength to flash out the other side of the transphasor. This is the transphasor's "on" state. In effect, this second, weaker beam exerts control over the strong one, very similar to a transistor, where a weak flow of electrons controls a strong one.

Several problems, however, still must be solved before transphasors will become practical. Currently, experimental transphasors require too much power. As the transphasors become smaller, power consumption and the amount of heat given off plummets. But as the size of the transphasors shrinks, it becomes difficult to accurately control the light beams for the transphasor. Researchers must juggle these variables of power, heat, and light to find a good equilibrium between them. Researchers working on the transphasor, working almost exclusively from Heriot-Watt University in Edinburgh, have led the drive into optical computing research. In 1985, Heriot-Watt University became the first European participant in SDI after being awarded a $150,000 contract to bring their results with the transphasor into commercial development.

The SEED

Coincidentally, when researchers at Heriot-Watt University first released their ideas on the transphasor in 1979, a group at Bell Laboratories simultaneously published a proposal for a related approach to optical switching. In June 1986, the Bell Labs team, led by Alan Huang, head of optical computing research department at Bell Labs, unveiled the first rudimentary solid-state optical chip. (Ironically, the chip was developed by David Miller, a member of the Heriot-Watt team in 1979.) Dubbed the Self Electro-Optic Effect Device (SEED), the SEED works by using an electro-optic effect, a phenomenon that occurs when an electrical field affects the optical properties of a material. In the SEED's case, when a voltage is applied, it becomes transparent, and allows a beam of light to shine through. When a second, less-powerful beam is directed at the SEED, the SEED's structure changes, and becomes opaque to light. This second, weaker beam controls the strong one, much like a conventional transistor.

The SEED consists of more than 2,500 alternating layers of gallium arsenide and gallium aluminum arsenide, each less than 10 atoms thick. On top of these layers lie supporting circuitry: the SEED requires an internal voltage and series of resistors. In its original state, the SEED is opaque to light, but its internal voltage makes it transparent and allows light to shine through. However, when a second beam of light enters, the SEED become opaque again and the internal voltage is redirected to and absorbed by the resistors. The entire device is only six micrometers, or six-thousandths of a millimeter thick.

Bell Laboratories and AT&T are particularly interested in optical computing for its possible applications in communications. As more and more of AT&T's telephone lines are replaced by fiberoptics, light, and impulses, the need for optical processors becomes apparent. These optical communications lines will be able to handle thousands of calls containing voice, data, and visual information simultaneously. David Miller, who designed the SEED, projects that a single optical chip could handle the traffic of all 5 billion inhabitants of earth talking simultaneously on the telephone. But optical computing does not end there. Alan Huang, the director of the Bell Labs effort describes it as "the first shot of a revolution."

The Josephson Junction

While semiconductor research continues to progress at a rapid pace, the evolution of semiconductor technology over the last 40 years has brought it to the physical limits of the universe in terms of transistor size, speed, and density. As a result, researchers are resorting to increasingly exotic ideas in their quest for progress. One of these technologies that had once shown great promise for the future is the Josephson junction.

The Josephson junction is a switching device unlike any semiconductor transistor, and has the potential to bring computer technology to new heights of advancement. The Josephson junction is capable of ultrafast speeds, 10 to 50 times faster than even the most nimble silicon transistors. Very significantly, the Josephson junction requires only a ten-thousandth of the power while producing a thousandth of the heat of conventional silicon transistors. Low power consumption and heat dissipation allow Josephson junctions to be packed together in incredibly high concentrations. All of this translates into a boon for the computer industry, and makes Josephson junctions ideal for computer use. Indeed, at one point, Josephson junction research involved such names as IBM, Sperry, Bell Labs, the University of California at Berkeley, TRW, and the National Bureau of Standards, and accounted for more than half of the funds allotted for semiconductor development in Japan.

The Josephson junction is a superconducting switch. Simply put, a superconductor is a very good electrical conductor. Josephson junctions are based on the Josephson effect, a rather paradoxical phenomenon involving superconductors first predicted by Brian Josephson in 1962. Josephson predicted that a spontaneous current would flow between two superconductors, even with no source of power. Although strange, the Josephson effect is very stable, and can be used to exhibit atomic constants in nature, which has led to its adoption as an international electrical standard. For his work in superconductors, Josephson, who was a graduate student at Cambridge University at the time, received the Nobel Prize in Physics in 1972.

In order to become superconducting, a substance must be cooled to temperatures as low as -270 degrees Fahrenheit, the temperature of liquid nitrogen. At these temperatures, substances lose all resistance to electrical current. But if a small amount of heat or a tiny magnetic field is added to a superconductor, a critical threshold will be reached and the substance will cease superconducting.

Inside the Josephson junction (FIG. 5-4), a tiny magnetic field is used to switch between its states. Two superconductors, usually made of lead or niobium, are placed next to each other and separated by a thin layer of insulation. A current begins to flow spontaneously between the two superconductors. This is the Josephson junction's "on" state. Above the two superconductors lies a control line, and a constant voltage flows through it. When this voltage increases, the magnetic field of the current also increases. When it reaches a critical threshold, the magnetic field causes the spontaneous current flowing between the two superconductors to stop. This is the Josephson junction's "off" state. In this way, the control line can switch the Josephson junction between these "on" and "off" states.

Although the Josephson junction promises a soaring increase in speed, recent advances in semiconductors and other microchip technologies have limited its improvements. In many cases, the cost of developing an entirely new technology such as the Josephson junction is not justified in comparison to improving existing semiconductor technologies. Indeed, in 1983, IBM, Sperry, and Bell Labs all decided to cut back their Josephson junction development in favor of other promising technologies, and the Japanese also have scaled back their Josephson junction research. The intense temperatures to which Josephson junctions must be exposed has proved to be a major stumbling block for

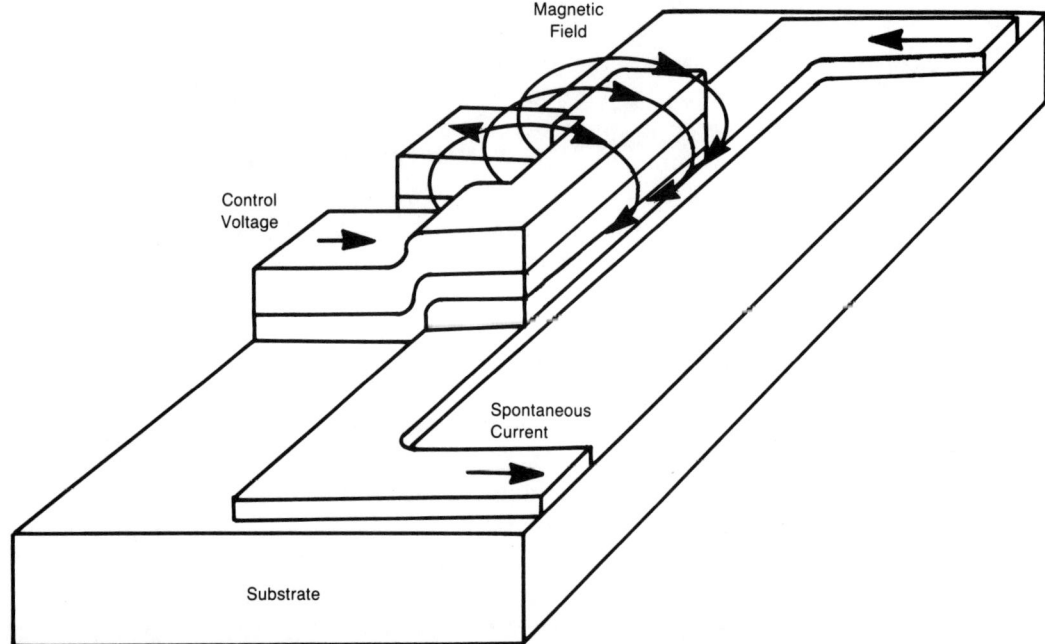

Fig. 5-4. The Josephson junction. The spontaneous current traveling through the lower wire can be switched on and off at will, according to control voltage above. The control voltage, upon reaching a certain threshold, creates a magnetic field that inhibits the flow of the spontaneous current, thus allowing the control voltage the ability to switch the Josephson junction on or off.

researchers. Recent improvements in superconductors have raised the temperatures needed to a very easily attained −30 degrees Fahrenheit. More improvements and advances might mark a resurgence of Josephson junction development.

Molecular Technologies

Imagine a supercomputer, implanted inside your head, powerful enough to act as your second brain, sorting through tedious data processing chores and freeing your mind for more creative tasks. Science fiction you might ask? Molecular technology might just turn that fiction into reality. For more than a decade, researchers have dreamed of a molecular computer, a product of genetic engineering, chemistry, and molecular biology. After all, molecules are very small, and in the computer industry, small is beautiful. A single molecular computer can have more than a million billion times the memory of supercomputers today, but be as large as a sugar cube. One molecular chip could have the capacity to store all the information ever recorded by mankind in a space the width of two human hairs. Indeed, the recent burst of interest in molecular computing has sparked an outbreak of advances being made by university, defense, and medical researchers.

EMV Associates of Rockville, Maryland, is working on a molecular chip covered by as many as 100,000 electrodes made from cultured nerve cells, which might restore sight to the blind. These cells could be attached to the visual cortex, and allow camera images to be directly given to the eye. Chemists at the University of Maryland and at Warwick University in Britain have announced that they are on the brink of several breakthroughs involving "molecular" transistors. Even the National Science Foundation has begun to step up its molecular research funding.

Forrest L. Carter, head of the molecular-electronics research project at the Naval Research Laboratory in Washington, D.C., envisions faster and cheaper computers more than a million times more powerful than supercomputers at present. At a workshop at the Naval Research Laboratory in 1983, perhaps the birthplace of the molecular computer, participants speculated on the future of molecular research.

Molecular Rectifier

One possibility presented at the workshop by researchers from the University of Mississippi is the molecular rectifier, an idea originally conceived in 1974 by researchers at IBM. A rectifier is a device that limits an electrical current to flow in one direction and one direction only. Currently, semiconductor rectifiers are used for everything from light sensors, lasers, voltage converters, and amplifiers to switching devices, computer logic circuits, and digital communication systems. A molecular rectifier would probably not only be smaller and faster, but require less power and generate less heat than conventional rectifiers.

The proposed molecular rectifier consists of three parts: two organic molecules and an insulating barrier separating them. These organic substances, usually tetrathiofulvalene (TTF) and tetracyanoquinodimethane (TCNQ), react with each other, and TCNQ attracts electrons away from TTF. Inside the molecular rectifier, the insulating barrier prevents this exchange.

The entire molecular rectifier can be likened to two cities, TTF on the west coast, and TCNQ on the eastern seaboard. Between the two cities is a very rapidly moving "jet stream" flowing to the east. A plane flying from TTF towards TCNQ finds that it has a very easy time, pushed by the wind going in the same direction. But if a plane attempts to fly from TCNQ to TTF, it must move against the wind, and encounters a great deal of resistance to its travel. Hence for all practical purposes, planes are limited to flying from TTF to TCNQ. Within the molecular rectifier, TCNQ exerts an attraction on TTF much like this "jet stream." Electrons find it much easier to flow from TTF to TCNQ than vice versa, and are thus limited to travel in only one direction.

Several problems currently prevent molecular rectifiers from being built. First is the problem of finding the best combination of molecules to form a molecular rectifier. Second, there is the problem of fabricating the rectifiers as organized layers of films. Third, small structures such as the molecular rectifier might be vulnerable to heat because excessive voltages or temperatures would fry an organic molecule.

However, another proposed idea might avoid these problems altogether—that idea is solitons. Solitons are waves and impulses that travel inside molecules like currents and signals, in a way very similar to how a pulse moves down a long spring. These currents are carried along molecular "wires," one-dimensional strings of the polymer transpolyacetylene, and are exploited to replicate the logic and memory functions of solid-state electronics. Many designs for memory elements, logic gates, soliton generators, and other molecular electronic devices already proliferate, although as of yet only experimental evidence exists supporting soliton theory.

The most difficult hurdle for solitons might not be solitons themselves but the molecules to hold them. Most of the molecules projected for solitons use have not been made yet, and present synthetic chemists with an overwhelmingly complicated and delicate task. Molecular fabrication might prove to be the most arduous obstacle standing in the way of molecular technology.

Photochromic Molecules

So far, photochromic molecules might be the most promising approach to molecular electronics. Photochromic molecules are sensitive to light, and exposure changes the molecule's structure. This change can be turned into a switching device, driven by light rather than electricity.

The closest thing yet to a molecular electronic device is an optically driven molecular switch developed by several researchers at the Johns Hopkins University Applied Physics Laboratory in Laurel, Maryland. This molecular switch consists of a thin polycrystalline film made of TCNQ in combination with copper and silver. A beam of laser light directed at the switch reduces its initially highly resistive state toward electrical current by a factor of over 10,000. Upon removal of the laser light, the highly resistive state is restored.

Other photochromic molecules might change color when irradiated with light. Research at the Universitat Stuttgart in West Germany is focused on photochromic molecules, specifically the molecule salicylidene aniline. Originally, salicylidene aniline is colorless, but turns red upon exposure to ultraviolet light. The ultraviolet rays cause hydrogen atoms to shift toward different regions of the molecule, resulting in a change in color. Visible light returns the red substance to its colorless form once again.

Photochromic molecules might have a new impact on data storage devices, in an application very similar to laser disks. A disk laden with photochromic molecules can be exposed to a laser beam that writes information on its surface. A second laser beam can read the information stored on the disk according to its color. Visible light will "erase" the data. Photochromic molecules will not have only the advantage of storing information with ten times the density of lasers disks, but can access the data in as quickly as one ten-trillionth of a second. High speed molecular disks would mean a quantum leap for data storage technology. Companies such as Hughes are busy developing molecular media technology. Commercial production of molecular storage media is slated within a year.

All the ideas discussed in this chapter have only one goal in mind: smaller, faster, better computers. Josephson junctions, SEEDs, solitons, photochromic molecules, and transphasors will all be a part of the fifth generation of tomorrow. Semiconductors, in spite of fierce competition from these technologies, will probably continue to dominate electronics.

Chapter 6
Speech Recognition

For decades, researchers have sought to find a way to interact with computers through the medium of speech. Because typing is such a slow, tiresome, and inefficient method of data entry—and many people would rather listen to a computer rather than read words from a screen—it seems logical that working with computers through human speech is a goal worth working toward. In past years, a great deal of work has been done in this area, and it has proved to be a much more formidable problem than it appears at first glance.

While it is relatively easy to get computers to speak our language, it is much more difficult to get them to understand our speech. Governments and private organizations have spent millions trying to develop a listening computer, a system that can accept input and understand it. The research being done in this area is the subject of this chapter.

Advantages of Speech Processing

Of course, the most obvious advantage of speech recognition is that people usually can speak faster and more easily than they can type. Speech is the most natural and prevalent mode of communications between people, and is probably the way that most people would like to communicate with computers. Just consider most of the people you know—how many would call you on the phone and talk rather than write you a letter? If effective speech recognition were perfected, it would open up the use of computers to many more people who now have a negative view of typing at a CRT terminal.

Speed is another obvious advantage in trying to get computers to speak our language. An average speaker can talk at least twice as fast as he or she can type, and of course speaking is relatively effortless in comparison to typing. Speech does not require physical or visual contact, and does not require the use of hands or the body. This is especially useful in situations where use of hands, eyes, and attention is critical, such as for pilots, drivers, business executives, and product assemblers. Clearly, speech is an important field for further research.

Applications

With the advantages of speech recognition clearly in mind, a discussion of viable applications is appropriate. The market for speech-related products is estimated to be quite large—in the area of $3.5 billion—however, developments in this area have been coming forth very slowly, and new products are being released very infrequently. The market at present is estimated to be only about $30 million, a fraction of its potential.

Some of the uses of speech systems include the following:

Remote Access Systems Computers can be accessed through the telephone through voice commands. You call up a system, say what information you want, and the computer will deliver your information verbally from its database.

Machine Operations Many machines that normally require manual operation can be worked with through speech commands. For instance, a car phone dials the number you want through spoken instructions, so that you need not dial the numbers yourself while driving.

Data Entry Entering information into a computer is a time-consuming task that often requires a staff of typists to handle. Speech-operated data entry makes the job much easier and faster.

Machines for the Handicapped Speech would be the right choice for improved access to computers and other machines for the handicapped, especially for those with limited mobility and use of their hands and fingers.

Automatic Dictation Dictating, transcribing, and preparing a letter is a long and time-consuming task. A system that understands speech takes dictation directly from the executive, and has it in printed form in seconds.

Voice Print Identification Featured in many science fiction movies, voice print identification is an effective and quick means of identifying someone through his or her unique pattern of speech.

Voice-operated Toys and Dolls Voice operated toys and dolls can understand when spoken to, and respond appropriately.

These are just some of the many uses for which speech systems can be implemented. In fact, speech systems are already in use at some factories for situations where workers cannot take their hands and attention away from a task—the so-called "hands-busy, eyes-busy" jobs. Although there is some use for speech systems for businesses, widespread use still is not prevalent.

The sheer number of important applications makes work in speech recognition a priority.

Some Background: Human Speech

Before tackling the methods in which speech systems work, it would be useful for you to understand how human speech works, and why the complexities of speech formation and understanding make it such a difficult task.

To start, whenever you speak, a flow of air from the lungs passes through the larynx, or voice box, into the throat, and out through the mouth. If the velum (flap of soft tissue at the rear of the palate) is lowered, the airflow also proceeds out through the nose; however, if the velum is raised, the nasal passages are blocked. To restrict the airflow, you can either press the tongue against the palate or close the glottis, which consists of two parallel folds of soft tissue (the vocal cords) within the larynx.

The vocal cords, which create the sound, can be made to vibrate much like the double reed of an oboe or bassoon. When the vocal cords are brought together, they stop the passage of air from the lungs and pressure builds up below them. The pressure forces the vocal cords apart, but the velocity of the rushing air then reduces the pressure in the space between the vocal cords. The reduction of pressure and the elasticity of the tissues bring the vocal cords together again, in position for another buildup of pressure. The rate at which this cycle is repeated is the fundamental frequency of the voice, which is heard as pitch.

The vocal tract can also form a constriction in the airway narrow enough to cause turbulence. For example, forcing air past a close contact between the upper teeth and the lower lip causes a turbulent flow that is perceived as the sound "f." Unlike the periodic sounds created by vibration of the vocal cords, the sounds generated by turbulent flow are aperiodic, or noiselike. It is possible for the vocal tract to create both aperiodic and periodic sounds at the same time. Combining vocal-cord vibration with the noise source of an "f" gives rise to the sound perceived as a "v."

Sound can be generated when pressure built up behind a closure is abruptly released. Such bursts of acoustic energy occur in the pronunciation of consonants such as "p," "t," and "k."

Sounds are shaped by the mouth, throat, and nose. Without passing through the mouth, throat, and nose, the sounds coming out of the vocal tract would sound rather like a door buzzer and not like speech at all. It is the shape of the vocal tract, including the positions of the larynx, the tongue, the lips, and the velum, that distinguishes, for example, the "ee" sound in "me" from the "oo" sound in "you."

With these concepts in mind, you can see that speech formation is a complex task, so getting a machine to understand it is even more difficult.

Problems in Speech Recognition

Speech recognition by a computer is made difficult by a variety of problems, the following of which are the most significant:

Coarticulation Coarticulation is when various sounds run into each other. The effect of this is to alter slightly the 40 or so phonemes (sounds) that make one word differ from another. Instead, the words appear as a continuum of sounds.

Speaker Independence Speaker independence problems occur because no two speakers sound alike. Two speakers, saying the exact same thing, differ in terms of the sound patterns they produce, whether in duration or in the distribution of energies across the range of frequencies in a spoken phrase.

Quality of Voice The sound of a person's voice depends on the way the person moves the tongue and mouth, as well as the unique arrangement and condition of the person's vocal cords. A person's voice can be described as being "croaky," "breathy," or one of other types.

Emotions, Accents, Emphasis, Pronunciation Other variants of speech that complicate the task of speech recognition include emotions, accents, emphasis, and pronunciation. One solution is to include alternate pronunciations in the device's "dictionary"; however, that would make the device have to recognize many more different sounds than the basic phonemes.

Context Words that sound alike, but are spelled differently according to context, are a problem. For instance, consider "to," "two," and "too." Similarly, a certain pattern of sounds can resemble two entirely different strings of speech. The two phrases "recognize speech" and "wreck a nice beach" can be made to sound virtually identical, and need to be identified via context. A word such as "bank" can be either a noun or a verb, depending on context.

How Speech Systems Work: Initial Analysis

Now that you understand how human speech works, and what problems the spoken word can cause for machines, it is time to examine how speech systems actually work. A given speech recognition machine might use one, several, or all of these techniques in order to understand speech. The first step is to analyze the incoming spoken information, a phase known as *initial analysis*.

There are three main techniques for initial analysis: filtering, zero-crossing count, and linear predictive analysis.

Filtering uses a bank of some 20 to 30 filters, each of which is tuned to a particular frequency. This set of filters in effect covers the frequency range of the human ear, and every 10 or 20 milliseconds captures the information that is sent through each filter, and the output of each filter is a measure of the energy in that frequency band. The output represents the digital representation of sound. The computer then compares this representation against digital patterns stored in its memory. The system's vocabulary is a collection of digital patterns, each representing a word, which were originally placed in memory by the operator speaking into the machine. To overcome variations in speech patterns is to use Markov modeling to analyze the same word being spoken many times, so that differences will not affect the analysis.

Zero-crossing count is a rather simple method that consists of counting the number of times the voltage analogue of the speech signal changes its sign from negative to positive (or vice versa) in a fixed interval of time. The number of crossings is related to its frequency, with the more crossings representing a higher frequency. This method is attractive because it requires rather simple electronic devices to operate.

Linear predictive analysis is a method that predicts the amplitude of a speech wave at a given instant from a weighted sum of its amplitudes at a small number of earlier instants. The coefficients, or weights, that give the best estimate of the true speech wave can be mathematically converted into an estimate of the amplitude spectrum. This can produce a smooth speech wave that approximates nonnasalized voiced speech.

Recognition Techniques

The next step is recognition of the speech, and this is a most crucial and difficult step. There are four main methods for speech recognition: direct template matching, dynamic programming, segmentation, and island driving.

Direct template matching involves comparing the words based on statistical closeness, and this is a rather difficult method to implement. The recognizer calculates the difference in space between the utterance and each template. Then, the template (or class of templates) closest to the spoken utterance is chosen to identify the word. This is effective for identifying single words; however, for a long portion of continuous speech, the ambiguity between word boundaries causes problems.

Dynamic programming was developed by Richard Bellman of the University of Southern California School of Medicine. The basic concept of this approach is to decide between several alternatives when it comes to recognizing a segment of spoken sound by using sounds recorded in memory. In other words because a person will never say a word in exactly the same way, there is a need to obtain the best fit possible between the spoken sound and those in the computer's memory by making variations to the input to make a clear match with recorded templates. Dynamic programming is the form of an algorithm, and can be used both for words and for phrases. In the latter case, the dynamic programming algorithm finds the sequence of isolated patterns in memory that most closely matches the phrase being analyzed. Together with rules of grammar, which specify the sequence in which words can appear, a reasonable understanding of the spoken passage is obtained.

Segmentation is another important technique for speech recognition. Because there are more than 300,000 words in English, far greater than that which can be reasonably tested using template matching, a better and simpler way is to look at the sounds, rather than the words.

In English, there are about 20,000 syllables, which is still a sizable number, so syllabic segmentation might not be practical. However, for a language such as Japanese, with only 500 or so syllables, segmenting syllables is a viable choice.

Another approach is to segment by phonemes. In English, these are basic linguistic elements, some 40 in all, such as vowels and consonants. For instance, there are three individual phonemes in the word *sit*, while "th" is another phoneme consisting of two letters. The identical letters can represent two different phonemes, such as "th" in *thy* and "th" in *thigh*.

An even deeper level is segmentation by phonemic unit. In this case, all phonemes can be broken down into about a dozen phonological features that specify vocal-tract shape and larynx control. With these phonemic units, the machine can be given rules for forming words, with consideration given for different pronunciations and speech variations of the same word.

In contrast to other methods, the task is not to identify each segment of sound, but rather to suggest the most probable sequence of sound patterns held in its memory to explain the spoken phrase. However, these patterns of sound are usually complex, abstract, and not well understood.

Island driving, not to be mistaken with visiting the Florida Keys, is the term for a method that selects the words in a sentence that are most likely to have been interpreted correctly. The program tries to connect these "word islands" by selecting the most likely interpretations of the remaining words with the previously interpreted words. This is a useful technique because in a given segment of speech, some words are enunciated clearly, while others are slurred.

These four techniques are the ones most widely used and studied among those involved with speech systems. The following sections examine existing speech systems and those being developed today.

Speech Systems and Research

The preceding sections discussed some of the background behind how speech is received, analyzed, and recognized. This section discusses the main speech projects and systems that have played a part in bringing us closer to a talking and listening computer.

Existing Systems

In 1971, DARPA instituted a five-year Speech Understanding Research (SUR) project. DARPA spent several million dollars developing ideas for speech recognition machines. Several organizations and universities took part, including SRI, Bolt, Bernandek, and Newman, and

Carnegie–Mellon University. The goal was to produce a system operating with less than 10 percent error with a limited domain of around 1,000 words. At the beginning of the project no system could recognize corrected speech, and individual word recognition systems could have only vocabularies of less than 100 words. However, steady development on the system continued until around 1976, after which followed about seven or eight years where very little work was done in the area.

One development of the program is the HARPY system, which could answer questions from a database. HARPY can identify words spoken by three male and two female speakers in a quiet room with an average error rate of two words out of every 100, boasting an overall 97 percent accuracy rate. The machine uses a network of speech-pattern templates to understand speech in a limited domain of 184 sentences. The network structure used by HARPY is equipped with syntax and semantics and can construct all the possible sentences that HARPY can understand. The speaker-independent (not trained for a specific user) HARPY uses a heuristic technique called beam search to prune unpromising paths from the network. As for understanding individual sound elements, a more specific task that could not use heuristics, HARPY was only 42 percent accurate.

Another machine developed at Carnegie–Mellon, HEARSAY, uses syllabic analysis and a knowledge of syntax and semantics to allow you to play chess against the computer using only spoken commands. Knowledge about the state of the game allowed HEARSAY-I to anticipate a range of next moves to be spoken by the human, limiting the range of possible words and statements of the system.

HEARSAY II, which is used for document retrieval, analyzes a sentence on several "levels" at the same time. The various analysis levels do not communicate directly with each other, but share their conclusions in common areas—called a *blackboard*—to come up with a final interpretation by "committee." This is a speaker-independent program, and had an accuracy rate of 90 percent.

Hear What I Mean (HWIM), developed in the mid-1970s by Bolt, Bernandek, and Newman, was designed to answer questions about travel expenses. HWIM includes phonemic representations of words likely to be encountered and implements rules that specify the way word combinations are spoken. This system achieves recognition accuracy of only 50 percent.

More Recent Developments

More recently, Logica, a British software company, developed one of the first commercial speech recognizers capable of recognizing connected speech. It was developed for Britain's Joint Speech Research Unit, housed at Government Communications Headquarters at Cheltenham. The system, called LOOPs, can instantaneously identify several hundred words stored in a vocabulary, and also holds simple grammatical phrases to increase the total size of the vocabulary and improve the accuracy of word recognition.

At IBM's Thomas J. Watson Research Center at Yorktown Heights in New York, the staff takes this approach of connected speech further. A machine developed by the Speech Recognition Group, under the direction of Frederick Jelinek, analyzes in segments lasting 10 milliseconds. These segments are compared against a set of 200 basic sounds derived from analyzing more than 27 million words taken from office memoranda and business letters and identified as fast as they are spoken. Each word in the "vocabulary" of the IBM "voice typewriter" is made up of these primitive sounds. The machine analyzes the probability of each of these sounds occurring. These sounds have been tuned and "prepared" in connection with the speaker, who must speak portions of text, for around 20 minutes, into the system. The system functions quite well considering it is basically an IBM-PC implanted with several special purpose circuit boards. Just a few years ago the same system required a mainframe computer and three specialized processors, and it could only support a 5,000 word vocabulary.

The performance of this "voice typewriter" is accurate about 96 percent of the time, and its 20,000-word vocabulary covers some 98 percent of all business correspondence. In fact, the overall error rate for several speakers tested is around 6.3 percent, a bit higher than the number of spelling mistakes made by a human secretary typing a letter. Clearly, this product is quite useful for businesses.

British Telecom, Logica, and the University of Cambridge are working on a talking train timetable system called VODIS that people can use to ask questions to and receive spoken responses over the phone. VODIS stands for Voice-Operated Database Inquiry System, which starts out a session by identifying itself and asking a question such as "which train do you want?"

Using a Logos speech analyzer, the system uses a stored set of grammar rules to deal with expected responses. By asking key questions, such as the places and times of arrival and departure, VODIS can identify the right train from the database.

The system works on a "frame" approach, where each frame contains information about a certain area of knowledge, such as "timespec" for times of departure and arrival. Each slot in the frame is filled in by extracting key elements from the spoken input, or asking for these specific facts. The unique part of this system is that VODIS moves with the conversation instead of merely dealing with a rigid set of questions and answers. For instance, it can ask "Were do you want to leave from?" and you respond "I want to leave from Cambridge." VODIS will extract the important points "where leave = Cambridge" and "when leaves = 9 o'clock." This information will be maintained in memory so that further questions such as "When is the train right before that one?" or "When does it arrive?" can be answered. The system also will ask questions to confirm information if anything is unclear. The system has been implemented and tested, and additional work is being done to handle poor telephone connections and coarticulation problems.

Raymond Kurzweil's work in the field of speech recognition also deserves mention. He is one of the major players in the voice system field, and his work posed enough competition to cause the Alvey project to drop further work in the field. Kurzweil is considered a genius in the computer field, with many accomplishments behind him. At age 13 he developed a statistical analysis program and sold it to IBM. Later, during his student years at MIT, he designed a system for matching students and colleges and sold it to a publisher for $100,000. Later, Kurzweil started his own company, Kurzweil Computer Products, which built a machine to read to the blind with a synthetic voice. He eventually sold the company to Xerox for $6 million. A couple years later, he started Kurzweil Music Systems, creating a keyboard instrument that almost perfectly simulated the sound of an acoustic piano.

In Summary

Speech technology is reemerging out of a slump and is a subject of great interest. Despite the wide market and somewhat "utopic" vision of a successful speech system, development has been slowed by various problems.

Additional work and research needs to be done in terms of signal analysis done by the ear, the relationship between sound symbols and actual sounds, syntax and semantics and their role in speech recognition, the process of language acquisition, and finally "adaptive abilities" that involve the key factors of training and experience. Computers that hold a basic set of expectations and abilities needed to learn a language need to be created. Neural networks might play an important role in this development. Speech recognition is definitely an important technology, and one that will be the subject of research and study for many years to come.

Chapter 7
Vision Systems

Vision is perhaps the greatest and most important of the human senses. While dogs and cats rely on their sense of smell, and bats and dolphins use their sense of hearing, human beings use their eyes. The world is inherently visual, packed with visual cues and signs from television, billboards, movies, paintings, and more.

Vision gives us, without conscious effort, detailed information about the shape of the world around us. "A picture is worth a thousand words" is an appropriate expression. In English, the idiom for "to understand" is "to see." Vision is equated with knowledge as in the expression "seeing is believing."

Vision is often taken for granted, however, because it is so effortless and automatic. It is not surprising that AI researchers in the early 1960s were overconfident about quickly "solving" the problem of vision. There were already many programs at the time that could play chess reasonably well, and vision appeared to be a much simpler, straightforward goal than a chess-playing computer. In fact, vision seemed so easy to those early AI researchers that legend has it that one graduate student was given just a single summer to create a visual computer system. Nobody knows what became of that hapless student that summer, but almost three decades later, vision remains one of the greatest challenges of artificial intelligence research.

The eye often has been compared to a camera, but it would be more appropriate to compare it to a TV camera attached to an automatically tracking tripod—a machine that is self-focusing, adjusts automatically for light intensity, has a self-cleaning lens, and feeds into a computer with parallel processing capabilities so advanced that engineers are only just starting to consider similar strategies for the hardware they design. By translating light into nerve signals, the eye begins the job of pruning what is useful in the external world and ignoring the irrelevant clutter it receives from the more than 125 million receptors in the retina. Before the image is passed through the optic nerve, more than 10 billion operations will have been performed in less than a second; nothing in existence on the planet can begin to rival the capabilities of the eye.

The Versatility of Vision

Human vision is versatile enough to deal with the almost infinite variation of possible objects in the world. When confronted with a real cat, a porcelain cat, and a cat made out of twisted pipe cleaners, our eyes enable us to recognize them all as cats. A cat on its side or purring directly in front of us is still a cat. A cat in a bright yellow room and a cat in a dark blue room are no problem to identify. Even from the barest sketch or incomplete drawing of a paw or a tail, we can tell it is a feline picture. When we see a cat on television, our eyes allow us to transform the two-dimensional dots from the screen into a perception of the three-dimensional world. No computer can match the flexibility of human vision.

Vision is now the most intensely studied sense in AI. Progress has been slow over the last 30 years, but the fifth generation promises spectacular results for the future. Vision is at its greatest turning point in its history.

The key is recognizing that vision is not a separate, independent function of a specific organ, such as bending an arm, but that vision is really an extension of the brain. Vision takes up more than 60 percent of the cerebral cortex, the center for all sensory processing. All of the other senses—taste, touch, hearing, and smell—must share the rest. Vision's scope overlaps with the area of symbolic representation in the brain, problem solving, and inference. As researchers delve further, computer vision eventually might shed some light onto the mysteries of animal vision by providing some fresh metaphors and perhaps a little insight into ourselves.

Vision Systems

Vision systems today are helping hundreds of products—everything from cars and submarine propellers to microchips, light bulbs, and frozen pizzas—to be made more cheaply, more accurately, and more safely than ever before. The potential for vision systems is almost unlimited.

Vision systems can do jobs that are too tedious for humans to perform consistently, such as identifying or inspecting parts on assembly lines or labels on bottles. Vision systems can inspect dangerous items, such as radioactive materials. Vision systems can confirm in seconds that the hundreds of microscopic connections on a semiconductor chip are intact.

Although the common conception might be that vision systems only exist in factories where they are coupled with robots on automated assembly lines, the fact is that a great deal of vision technology has been in widespread use for years. The bar code readers at the supermarket are a good example. They are spinoffs from image processing, which uses rudimentary vision abilities for such diverse tasks as digital video, satellite surveillance, and weapon guidance. The image processing field is so commonplace today that it is no longer even considered a part of vision but a narrow discipline of electronics.

More advanced vision systems will arrive on the market out of the laboratories as the industry rides the wave of cheaper computer processing and meets the growing American demand to automate as a result of pressure from foreign competition. The vision industry is deceptively easy to enter because of its low capital costs and its obvious importance to the future. By 1990, annual sales of vision systems are expected to top $1.2 billion. But the industry is a crowded one, beset with marketing and production difficulties.

More than 80 companies, mostly less than 7 years old, court potential customers with a bewildering array of technological approaches to vision in the factory. That is a reduction: more than 200 companies crowded the machine vision field in 1985.

It is the same cycle as the initial boom in personal computers—companies racing to manufacture goods for a booming market, a price war wiping out profit margins and driving out many, and a subsequent series of mergers, partnerships, and failures leaving a leaner, but stronger pack of companies.

Even these winners face the costs of adapting cutting-edge technology to the gritty world of the factory. The practical problems usually are more than the optimistic investors and entrepreneurs who jumped the bandwagon ever estimated. Certain operations, such as welding, which is as much an art as a science, are very difficult to automate. Vision systems designed on paper often are unworkable because actual factory practice is much more complicated. There is worker resistance to the new technologies, because workers are worried about job security. Even worse, management does not understand the new machines being brought in.

No general vision system has been designed, the reason being the high costs of developing vision technology—the great deal of computer programming and engineering involved. A single demonstration alone can cost more than $20,000 to set up. The strategy that seems to work best is to focus on narrowly defined applications where a lot of information is known and technology can be applied with a minimum of modification. Successful vision systems are generally very specific solutions, tailor-made for the process.

A good example is a conveyor belt carrying known parts. At its Hamtramck plant in Detroit, General Motors uses machine vision for car body measurement. Approximately 130 cameras record 586 measurements of gaps and contours in metal parts in just 20 seconds. The same job used to require removing the sample car body from the assembly line and giving two men most of a day to test it with handheld gauges. Now the assembly can be adjusted much faster, and produce higher rates of quality.

The kind of products being applied on the factory floor represent 20-year-old ideas. There is another 20-year backlog of techniques waiting for the appropriate order of magnitude improvement in computers to come from the fifth generation. Will these breakthroughs make it to everyday environments without a lot of costly engineering and redesign? This "robustness question" is first on the vision industry's agenda.

Computer Vision Technology

Computer vision technology is under increasing refinement in the labs; it might be as close as AI has yet come to being a true science. The "low-level," or "early" part of the vision problem, which tries to identify primitive features of the image such as motion and boundary lines, is pretty much on its way to a systematic solution. The current state of the art within vision labs has built upon 30 years of vision research and is now approaching the 3-D level of perception—the final hurdle for vision.

The first attempts at vision during the 1950s were aimed at the simple recognition of two-dimensional images, such as the alphabet. Researchers relied on comparisons between unknown patterns and previously digitized patterns in computer memory for identification. Pattern recognition was essentially a statistical process that depended on the numerical analysis of the brightness intensities of each image versus those of the "template." Every pattern in the system's memory was compared to the unknown image and its degree of similarity calculated. The pattern that matched most closely was assumed by the machine to be the correct identification. The approach worked as long as the number of stored patterns was kept at a minimum. For larger groups of patterns, the system became hopelessly bogged down.

Although pattern recognition proved to be a failure as a substitute for animal vision, it allowed digital image processing technology, then in its infancy, to be perfected and developed more completely. This led the way, during the 1960s for the first attempts at true computer vision and "understanding" of images in complex 3-D scenes.

By the 1960s, the computational complexity of vision became apparent. Researchers began to write vision programs in earnest, only to discover that vision was a horrendously difficult task. Most of the researcher's work was directed at defining object boundaries, until it was found that boundaries were more than often simply a construct of the mind. The systems that were created proved unreliable and inadequate in dealing with the ambiguities and subtleties of images.

Researchers counterattacked by injecting domain-specific knowledge into their systems, to help prune out all the "impossible objects" that could never exist in three dimensions. The massive amounts of processing for a cognitive approach such as this one became economically possible during the 1970s. *Knowledge-directed vision*, as it was called, put a constraint on the realistic ways that lines, edges, and surfaces could meet, and used this geometric information to correctly identify blocks through logical analysis without having to match them with templates first. These systems used facts about gravity, support, occlusion, and spatial relationships to obtain their conclusions, but worked only in certain, narrow domains such as office scenes or polyhedral blocks that were highly simplified for the real world.

Much of computer vision's current state, and its understanding, is the result of a single influential figure—David Marr of MIT, whose career was cut short in 1980 by his death from leukemia at age 35. Marr became a pioneer by being one of the first to combine computational AI/vision research with results from experimental psychology, and his terminology is now standard in the field. While David Marr's contributions to vision are many, his greatest is his injection of science into the arena—letting people realize that early vision is really a science, as opposed to just a lot of ad hoc ideas.

According to Marr, whose theories were posthumously published in his enormously influential *Vision* in 1982, the first task of any successful vision system is to identify surfaces with definite positions and orientations in space before jumping to identifying any objects. This idea was not so groundshaking—vision systems in existence already made surface determination a priority. However, Marr drew a sharp distinction between his approach and the then popular *segmentation* methods, which tried to identify objects based on areas of equal shading or intensity in the image and analyzing the blobs. Segmentation fails miserably though when images do not contain all but the most dramatic boundaries or when they contain confusing factors such as reflections or shadows. Marr argued that identifying surfaces first was the best way to avoid these illusions.

The general formula of Marr's solution to the vision problem was in three distinct stages: two dimensional, two-and-a-half dimensional, and three dimensional. The goal in the early stages of the vision process is to get useful information from the raw image—as much as can be extracted without identifying the image outright. In later processing, this useful information will be incorporated with real world knowledge to determine what the image is.

The vision system receives an image as a collage of thousands upon thousands of dots made up of varying shades of gray. While the array is only an approximation of the original object, it is the easiest way for the computer to handle the information, which is stored in a database as a group of cartesian coordinates and corresponding gray level values. The artificiality of dissecting an image into a series of numbers is quite reasonable in comparison to the retina, which performs a similar operation at the back of the eye. People do not sense any reduction in their visual capabilities because the retina contains 100 million receptors to capture enough light to capture any image with reasonable accuracy. The image in the retina is still a series of dots; the retina cannot distinguish any image that is smaller than one of its receptors.

The first step in visual processing, the two-dimensional stage, is the production of the *primal sketch*, a description of edges and other parts of interest in the image. Getting to the primal sketch means filtering out noise from the raw data while simultaneously enhancing any recognizable features (FIG. 7-1). The refined scene becomes almost nothing but strokes outlining the original.

The primal sketch has the advantage of being easier to work with than the raw image. There is less data and less ambiguity; the primal sketch retains only the most important features of the image. While a single pixel from the original image could belong to anything at all, the primal sketch groups all the pixels together to form a more meaningful representation.

Determining the boundaries of an image for the creation of primal sketch, or *edge detection*, as it is often called is perhaps the most thoroughly studied process of vision. It is the area that has made the

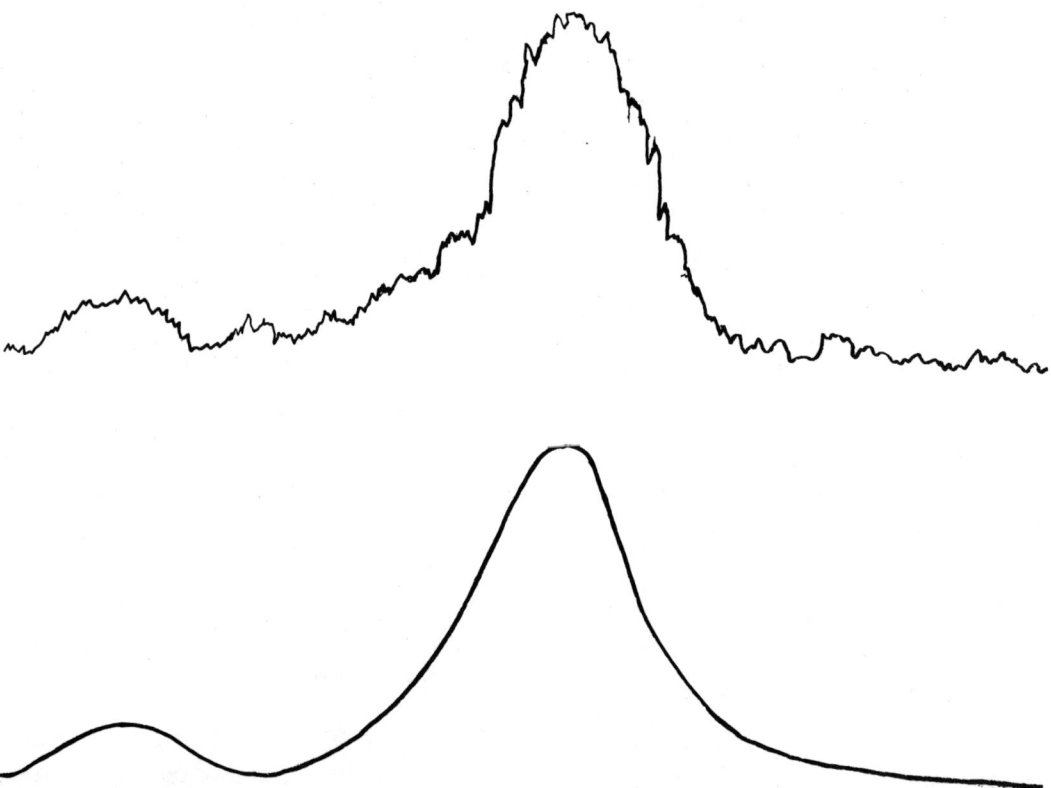

Fig. 7-1. Vision signal processing. A typical input signal, as shown above, will be rampant with irregular peaks and valleys that obscure the general shape of the curve. Constant smoothing techniques and other mathematical transforms turn the shape into a more usable one for further analysis. By doing so, the computer can ignore small irregular details that are a result of lighting or imperfections in structure, and emphasize the greater image.

most remarkable progress during vision's short history. Ideally, edge detection should deliver a line drawing of the scene that captures the physical contours and boundaries of the objects and leaves blank the surface in between. Five years ago, extracting edges from an image took 30 minutes of computer time; now it takes less than a tenth of a second and produces a clean enough image that can guide "smart" missiles to their target.

The greatest difficulty in edge detection is not so much finding the edges, but discarding the unimportant information and clutter. No image is perfect; even a sheet of plain white paper will register varying values of brightness across its surface when it should be uniform at every point.

The most successful edge detector is the Gaussian filter, modeled on human retinal cell's operation. (A Gaussian curve is the familiar "bell curve" used to illustrate probability and statistical distribution.) The filter eliminates spurious noise from the image by "smoothing" it out from its neighbors through the constant averaging of each point (FIG. 7-2). First, the filter blurs the area to be smoothed by adding values to the particular cluster. Then, the filter takes the average of the points,

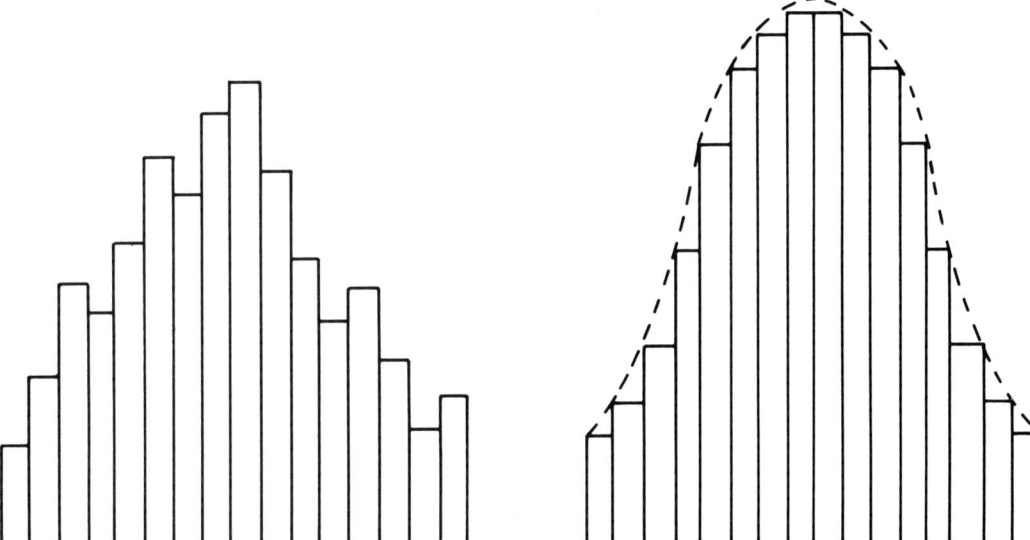

Fig. 7-2. A closer look at vision signal processing. The input signal's values can rest over a broad spectrum of numbers that are worthless on an individual scale. But when each value is analyzed in relation to its neighbors and accordingly altered, a more helpful shape is obtained.

ensuring that small changes in intensity are smoothed away and that large features are preserved. Miscellaneous lines are discarded through repetition.

By widening or narrowing the scope of the Gaussian filter's effects, the resolution of the resulting primal sketch can be controlled. If the resolution is too low, the smoothing will be much less effective; if the resolution is higher, there is the risk that some real edges will be smoothed away along with noise.

Once the primal sketch is in hand, "natural constraints" that attempt to reduce the ambiguity of the images and the number of possible interpretations are applied. These assumptions about the properties of lighting, motion, and geometries rule out the physically impossible and add to the information known about the scene. No judgments are made yet as to the nature of the image at this point, and no attempts are made to divide the scene into its individual component objects.

After the two-dimensional stage, scientists are much less sure about how to address the vision problem. It is obvious that in the last stage of vision processing, high-level, real-world knowledge must be injected into the scene in order to begin recognizing objects; it is less obvious as to how scientists can bridge the gap between edges and the final identification. Experimental evidence is lacking. The question about how to make the two halves of vision meet in the middle is still unanswered.

This halfway point, called the two-and-a-half dimensional sketch, takes the lines extracted from the scene in the first stage and connects them to form a representation of the surface involved. The goal is not to tell where things are or what they are, but to determine how they are. Facts about surfaces are explicit in the two-and-a-half dimensional sketch; orientation is noted, as well as surface texture, distance, brightness, and shape.

In human vision, special cells within the retina note such features as texture and shape. These cells are especially attuned to their particular task, and are very sharp perceptors of visual cues in images. Sometimes these visual cues are false and misleading—then we say we have an optical illusion. FIGURE 7-3 has two optical illusions. In FIG. 7-3A it is almost impossible not to perceive a white square outlined in the image—the eye automatically connects the blank spaces and short lines based on the subtle cues of the drawing. The white square even seems to cover another square beneath.

Fig. 7-3. Optical illusions. Although the human eye has no difficulty perceiving the implied shape of the square in A or the rough texture of the surface in B, these kinds of of optical illusions, which are intangible physically, are among some of the most puzzling aspects of vision research today. Scientists are at a loss as to how to mimic the human eye's capabilities.

FIGURE 7-3B has a three-dimensional quality of texture to the image, even though it obviously is flat. The orderly, repetitious pattern fools the eye into perceiving surface qualities that are nonexistent.

While the human eye has specialized cells to supply information on shape, texture, color, and orientation, computer vision relies on the primal sketch for its data; the primal sketch is the best condensation of the original image and its characteristics. To determine distance, for example, a stereo-vision procedure compares left and right primal sketches of the scene. Equivalent points in the two images are identified, and a rough match is made. Then it is only a case of simple mathematics to determine the distance. By using the primal sketches, the system reduces the chance for ambiguity or mismatch between the images; however, many details that might be helpful in aiding the process also are left out.

Although a great deal of progress is being made at all levels of vision, a number of difficult problems remain, especially at the level of the two-and-a-half dimensional sketch. What kind of surface information does the eye extract from a transparent windowpane or from the reflections of a pool of water? What does the eye do with a bank of fog or a curl of smoke, which do not even have surfaces?

The problems for vision become more apparent at higher levels. The goal of the three-dimensional stage of vision is to determine how the objects of the scene fill space and to begin identifying them. But before a program can recognize a three-dimensional object, or reason about it, that program first must have something in memory for comparison.

Knowledge representation is the ubiquitous black hole in all areas of AI. While introspection offers some partial hints as to how the brain organizes its information, such high-level activities are far less accessible to experiment than early vision, and thus there is far less guidance as to where to proceed.

The internal representation of objects that exists inside the brain is specific enough that any typical human being has no trouble distinguishing a person from a monkey, even though here are many similarities. But the representation is also general enough that a person can recognize a mannequin, a sculpture, a stick-figure, and a real human all at the same. Is there a single, empirical representation of a person in everyone's mind? A generic human being? Researchers can only conjecture; the fact is that no one has yet come up with a satisfactory explanation for the infinite versatility of the human mind.

The most common approach to representing objects from a scene in computer memory is to generalize them as combinations of cylinders, cones, rectangles, and spheres. This "block world" then becomes a crude approximation of the real objects it represents. The machine's task is made much easier by the fact that it is no longer working with a real image, but an intrinsic one. By transforming the symbolic representation in storage, the vision system can adapt to variations of the same object without any difficulty.

FIGURE 7-4A shows a line drawing of a pyramid in Egypt. The "block world" representation of the image is in FIG. 7-4B. The pyramid is reduced even further into a "stick" figure—a two-dimensional triangle in FIG. 7-4C. While each drawing is successively less detailed, each still suggests the original image from the qualities retained.

There is some evidence that the human visual system operates similarly to the "block world." The fact that a crude stick figure can still be recognized by a person demonstrates that even this basic form preserves the characteristics necessary for identification. Details are relatively unimportant.

Computer Vision Technology 103

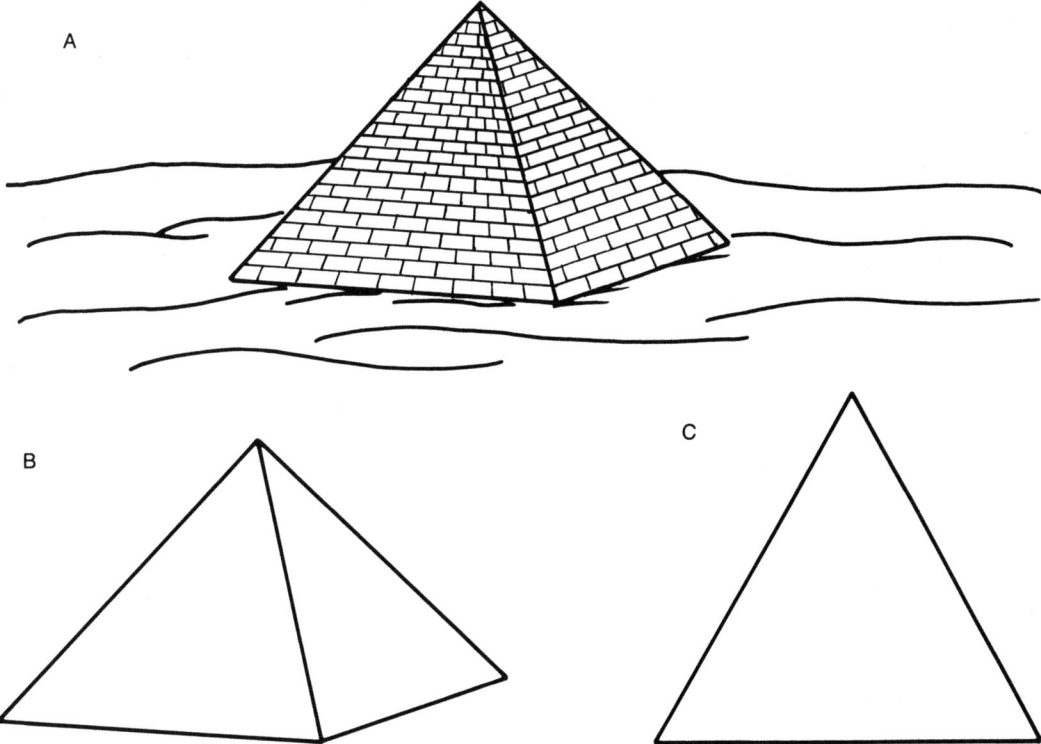

Fig. 7-4. Knowledge representation. A typical input scene, such as this one of a desert pyramid (A), is gradually reduced to more simple representations that the computer can understand. First, all extraneous scene details are removed and the major "actors" of the image are transformed into geometric shapes (B), then these three-dimensional shapes are reduced to even simpler two-dimensional transforms (C).

A great debate still rages among vision researchers about the proper way as to how information from one stage of vision processing should influence the other. A "bottom-up" organization is constructed like a pyramid. At the bottom is the raw data received from the image. As the computations continue, the system gradually focuses on the object's identity by using the results from each immediately preceding stage. This is most similar to the outline for vision processing proposed by David Marr.

In a *heterarchial constraint propagation*, information flows in all directions as the image is attached from every side. The free exchange helps different parts of the vision process narrow the possible choices in hand, based on the findings of other modules. By throwing all its expertise into a scene simultaneously, a heterarchial system tries to improve its chances for identification; too often, the result is confusion.

Other vision systems use *controlled hallucination*, a method where the system is guided by firm expectations about what is to be seen. Generally, this approach works only in narrow, constrained environments, where the system's scope is limited. Although such machines might be good enough for an assembly line, they are still far from the general vision machines that humans are, and that scientists are after.

After so many years, the only evident conclusion is that vision does not reduce to the equivalent of a series of computer codes. While genuine progress in vision has been slow in coming, new forces are at work that promise to speed up the pace considerably.

The latest trend in vision is more direct modeling of the physiological processes of animals, including neural structures. The general consensus among vision researchers is that the gap will not be bridged by more complex software, but by closer mimicry of animals' neural hardware. Scientists are finally taking a hint from nature and the complex interconnections of neurons in the brain. It is a big shift—AI revels in algorithms and programs; the new connectionism insists that hardware contains the essence that AI has failed to recreate.

Machine Vision

In a landmark paper entitled "What the Frog's Eye Tells the Frog's Brain," researchers at MIT reported in 1959 that the eye does not merely record an image, as film does, and pass it along to the brain for analysis, but rather the retina in the eye of both frogs and people sifts the information, rearranges it and sends only what is useful through the optic nerve. For instance, the nerve cells in a frog's retina mainly pick out small, dark, moving objects—potential food.

Shortly after the paper was released, scientists at RCA Laboratories built a frog retina as part of an effort to develop a robot with human capabilities. The retina measured 40 inches by 40 inches. The project was abandoned soon afterward.

The retina is a marvel. It is less than a centimeter square in a human eye and is made up of several layers of cells that receive the light. Almost automatically, the retina counteracts the effects of different intensities of light. Therefore we can recognize a tennis racquet both in a dimly lit room and at a bright beach. While that might seem trivial, machine vision systems can be thrown off by the slight difference between fluorescent and incandescent lighting.

The retina automatically compares points in an image with surrounding ones, locating the edges of objects. It has also been discovered that the retina's neurons contain "feature detectors" for say, line orientation, color, and motion. This discovery during the early 1960s later won David Hubel and Torsten Wiesel, both of Harvard, a Nobel Prize.

While much about the retina still remains a mystery, the advent of parallel processing and microchip technology has caused a resurgence of interest into building an artificial retina once again. Vision researchers will no longer write long computer programs as they did during the 1970s, but will actually try and create artificial visual parts.

Dr. Carver Mead of CalTech has already created an artificial retina, called the RET-30, and formed a company, Synaptics, Inc., to pursue his neural work. Conventional machine vision relies on constant comparison to detect motion, using complex mathematics to figure out which new point corresponds to which old point. The RET-30 works like an eye. Its circuits will retain an image, detect motion, and continually track the rate at which the image changes. It can follow the movements of a rotating fan, an almost impossible task for a conventional vision system. However, the RET-30 can only detect motion. If the fan is stationary, the chip will not see it. However, at two square inches, the RET-30 is evidence as to how far technology has come.

In another experiment, Dr. Ralph Linsker of IBM's Thomas J. Watson Research Center in Yorktown Heights, NY, constructed a neural network to investigate more exactly how the visual system develops its "feature detector" capabilities.

Using a simulation in which simplified neurons were connected more or less at random, Dr. Linsker showed that under certain conditions feature detectors would automatically emerge. Although it does not prove that the brain works precisely in this fashion, it does show the possibility for visual circuitry to be modeled on a computer.

As these models get more advanced, the situation could reverse itself. Scientists might construct their own sophisticated neural networks of the visual system, then turn to the anatomists and ask them if they have turned up clues that such networks actually exist.

The connectionists predict that the right hardware will spontaneously—if not magically—organize itself into an intelligent, working system. A single molecule bouncing off the walls of a container is nothing, but a hundred million molecules in motion create sound. A single neuron is but a cell, but billions of them working together form a brain. The connectionists are looking for emergent intelligence to appear once the right threshold is breached. Give the system the correct images with the correct answers and perhaps it will teach itself. How the system does it is of no importance.

Some critics argue that imitating nature is not always the best approach. If it were, cars would have legs and airplanes would have wings that flap. Very often, animals have developed good solutions to problems, but are not the most efficient model to choose from. The human eye is an example. The eye's circuitry has evolved into a very good detector for objects moving away and toward it—an atavism to man's early hunting days—but this adaptation is not necessarily useful for a task such as reading.

A traditional computer deals with extremely well defined inputs and well defined outputs. That is very different from the "fuzzy" tasks in most of the world that cannot be defined in simple ones and zeroes. Perhaps nature can offer the vision researchers some insights into the problems they face; they finally realize that artificial vision can gain much by emulating their biological counterparts that perform so extraordinarily well. It is hoped that the computer scientists will be able to repay their debt to biology someday.

Artificial vision might be the most important step in the evolution of AI. The ability to see and interpret the world around us is so integral to the human experience. Vision overlaps so many of the functions of the brain that it is doubtful that the problem of vision could be solved without at least understanding more about how the brain works.

For example, animals with vision develop motor systems, yet current research assumes that vision is logically disassociated from motor capabilities. Are the two systems linked? Can they be constructed independent of one another?

Until the eventful day that true artificial vision is produced, people should not shy away from the computer scientists who wish to duplicate their functions on machines. Man and his abilities are a constant reminder about how far nature has come and how far science has yet to go.

The future is bright. The advent of fast, massively parallel computers and vision's current leap into connectionism will no doubt help vision's progress. New funding from the Strategic Computing Initiative promises to bring new money and new energy into the field. Although no breakthroughs are guaranteed, building on a base of mathematics, engineering, psychology, neuroscience, and technology, people will continue to develop the powerful hardware, software, and theories with which to explore the mysteries of vision. The whole effort is not to create a man-machine, but to let man learn more about himself.

Chapter 8
Robotics

Robots have fascinated people for centuries. The idea of machines that can perform tasks, talk, move about, and even think have always been a part of man's dreams, imagination, and creative goals. Whether they be the Star Wars creations R2D2 and C3P0, the personal robot Hero 1, or the industrial robots in use today, robots are an important part of our computer age.

The desire for robots that can fulfill our every wish goes back a long way, long before we entered the computer age. From Mary Shelley's novel *Frankenstein* (1818) to Karel Kapek's play "R.U.R." (Rossum's Universal Robots, 1920), as well as Isaac Asimov's now famous Three Laws of Robotics from his book, *I, Robot* (1950), the idea of machines that can serve man by duplicating many of his physical capabilities has been a sought after goal. Just think of all the science fiction stories, programs, and movies you've seen—how many have featured some kind of robot?

Although personal robots, such as those most commonly imagined when the word *robot* is mentioned, are not yet available, robots have been in use in manufacturing and industry for some years now, performing tasks such as welding, assembly, painting, and machining. Many of these tasks are dangerous for people to perform, but robots can do them with hardly any risk at all.

What exactly is a robot? Actually, the entire class of machines generally classified as *robots* is known by several names, including automatons, androids, cyborgs, and of course, just plain robot. The word automaton is derived from the Greek words for "self" and "move," and is defined as a self-moving machine. Later the term automation was extended to mean machines constructed to imitate the form and motion of men and animals. The term robot was in fact introduced by Karel Kapek in his play "R.U.R.," which portrayed the creation of artificial persons who were efficient but devoid of sensitivity. Androids are man-made machines built in the form of humans; however, they appear in form and function to be somewhat "human." Cyborgs, on the other hand, like the "Six Million Dollar Man," are actual persons who have been fitted with some electronic or mechanical device to take the place of biological organs and limbs.

The modern, functional definition of robot is of a programmable machine that can manipulate and move objects through programmed motions for a variety of tasks. Because most of the robots in use today are industrial in form and nature, that will be the focus of this chapter.

Why Use Robots?

Before any kinds of robots were invented, everything was done by hand or through the use of standard machinery. Why should we use robots to do various tasks?

The answers are quite simple. Robots, like computers, are tireless and can dramatically improve productivity over strictly human effort. A robot can perform a task over and over, for hours on end, without tiring or requiring a rest period. Robots require only the minimum of maintenance and power in order to function, and can do a uniform job on every item worked on. High labor costs and demands for better benefits are other reasons why robots are being used to perform many industrial tasks.

Another important factor is safety. Many industrial jobs are quite dangerous, whether they involve heavy objects, high temperatures, toxic chemicals, high levels of noise, or handling explosive, or delicate materials. Robots can handle these tasks and spare people from the problems associated with these hazards.

Applications of Industrial Robots

Robots can be equipped and programmed for a variety of tasks, and it is this versatility that makes robots sought after in the area of manufacturing. Often a team of robots can be set to a task, such as assembling computer boards or putting together the body of an automobile with only a bare minimum of supervision. Here is a sampling of the many tasks that robots can do:

Welding

Welding is one of the most frequent uses of robots, and one that involves a set of computer arms set up along a conveyer belt, each programmed for a specific task. As soon as specified components are put into place, the robot arms move in to make welds at the required locations. Auto bodies and frames are commonly made using robot welders.

There are two main types of welding done by robots—spot and arc welding. Spot welding involves taking two pieces of metal, putting one atop the other, and fusing them at a single place, hence the name spot welding. Arc welding is used where joining is desired along a long path between two pieces of metal. A current is passed through a piece of tungsten wire and brought close to the surface creating a spark or "arc." Some inert gases are used to assume a tight bond and prevent oxidation, and the resulting heat melts the edges of the metal sheets, joining them together. This method has been used to make axle housings, as well as other robots.

Materials Handling

Heavy and dangerous parts can be moved easily using robot arms. Whether loading, unloading, transferring parts from one place on a conveyer belt to another, or picking parts out of a bin, robots can be programmed for the job. Robots are often used for putting on and taking off parts from pallets. Robot arms can exert either gentle or heavy force on an object, depending on its weight and other factors. A related task is that of loading and unloading parts to and from machines. This is common for such applications as die casting.

Assembly

Assembly applications differ from welding in that parts are joined using nuts, bolts, screws, or some other means. Assembly requires detailed, precise work that needs to be done accurately and quickly. Besides assembly of car and machinery components, the assembly of circuit boards is becoming an important task for robots. Robot arms pick up integrated circuits, memory chips, and other components and insert them into printed circuit boards. These boards are then sent down the line to be soldered.

There are several assembly-oriented robots that have been developed, including Unimation's Programmable Universal Machine for Assembly (PUMA), the Japanese Selective Compliance Assembly Robot Arm (SCARA), Olivetti's Sigma, and DEA's Pragma. The PUMA has worked on assembly tasks such as appliance and electrical component insertion. SCARA primarily is used for appliance assembly, such as for television sets and optical equipment parts. Pragma is significant because it has a tactile sensor and can in a sense "feel" if some part is in a wrong position or is defective. Olivetti's Sigma robots have vision capabilities that allow it to assemble circuit boards, and components for typewriters, pistons, and shock absorbers.

Spraying

The most common spraying application is painting, and it includes spray painting car bodies, machinery, and other parts. The robot arm has a special nozzle that can be made to spray a portion accurately, even if the shape of the object is very unusual. Enamel, oil, and polyurethane are other substances that are spray-finished on surfaces. The job, which was originally done by hand, is extremely toxic and dangerous to people, and the use of robots has made the entire process not only less dangerous, but also produces better results. Spray-finishing robots are "taught" to perform certain motions and control the paint stream to produce the best possible results.

Machining

Machining includes a variety of tasks, including grinding, cutting, polishing, drilling, sanding, buffing, deflashing, and deburring. Because this is a precise task, robots frequently need templates to guide them in the process.

Inspecting

Inspecting is another task that robots can do. For instance, an inspection system known as Autovision, developed by Automatix, uses a vision system to inspect products using three-dimensional readings and statistical analysis. It can detect the gaps in car subassemblies and communicate to other machines and robots earlier on that line whether or not the gap is too tight or too loose.

Robots are also used in situations far too hazardous for humans. Robot arms are used to handle radioactive fuel and wastes, miners use them to dispose of mineral wastes, sea salvages are accomplished through the help of robotics, and the robotic arm on the space shuttle can be used to launch a satellite.

Automobile manufacturing has been the one industry where the most robots have been bought and used, especially in Japan and the United States. Welding and machine loading and unloading and spray finishing are the tasks more commonly assigned to robots.

Other industries that are employing robots include the foundry industry, plastic manufacturing, cosmetics, and pharmaceuticals, electronics, and aerospace. Increased use of robots and further growth in the field are expected.

How Do Robots Work?

To many, robots seem to work as if by magic. They are "intelligent" machines that seem to do their tasks without much instruction or guidance. In reality, however, robots are complex and require a great deal of guidance to "teach" them how to perform their tasks.

In fact, even the simplest of industrial robots consists of a number of parts, all of which need to be controlled and directed by a computer or controller device. The main components of a robot that will be discussed here are the manipulator arm, end effector, actuator, and controller.

Manipulator Arms

The manipulator arm resembles, at least in general form, the arm of a human. The arm can be moved around in various ways to provide for flexibility, and there are five different kinds of arms that are available.

The *cartesian* or *rectangular coordinate arm* is probably the simplest in form, and the idea is to move the arm around to perform some kind of task. The points to which it can move are governed by the X, Y, and Z axes of the cartesian coordinate system, the familiar grid-like system you probably learned in high school algebra. The motions are basically right-to-left, up-and-down, and forward-and-backward. See FIG. 8-1 for an illustration of a cartesian coordinate arm.

The *cylindrical coordinate arm* is a variation of the cartesian arm and while it can move in much the same way as a cartesian arm, it also

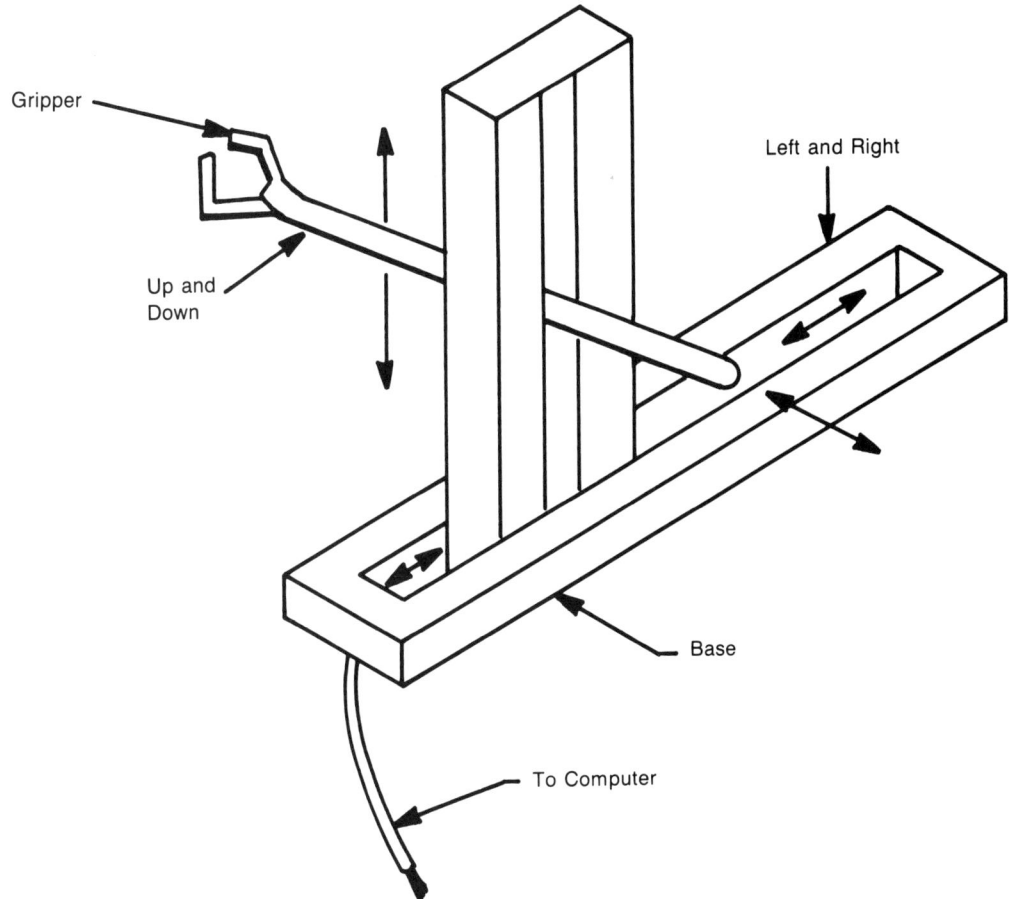

Fig. 8-1. Cartesian coordinate robot arm. This shows the components and operation of a cartesian coordinate arm.

can rotate about its base 360° instead of movements along the X axis. This gives additional flexibility to the arm. See FIG. 8-2 for an illustration of a cylindrical coordinate arm.

The *spherical* or *polar coordinate arm* adds another dimension to the versatility of robot arms, with the addition of a shoulder joint that allows for the arm to tilt upward and downward, in addition to the base rotation and other motions. It can perform elevation or pitch to reach straight above or to either side. See FIG. 8-3 for an example of a spherical coordinate system.

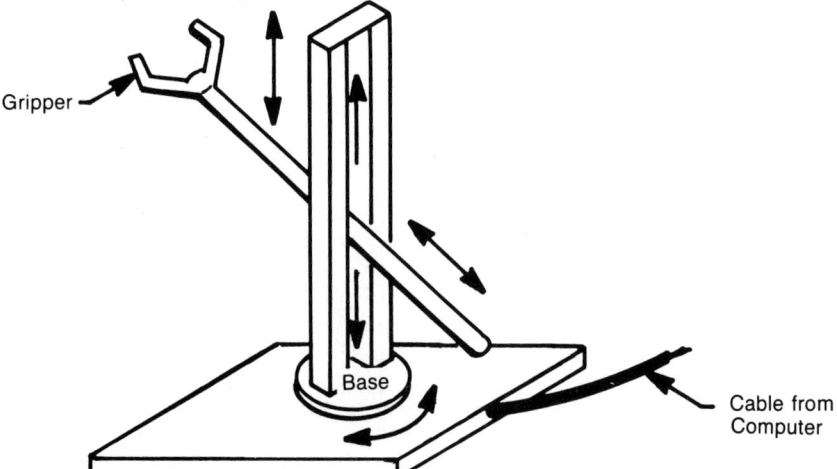

Fig. 8-2. *Cylindrical coordinate robot arm. This shows the major parts and components of a cylindrical coordinate arm, and how it works.*

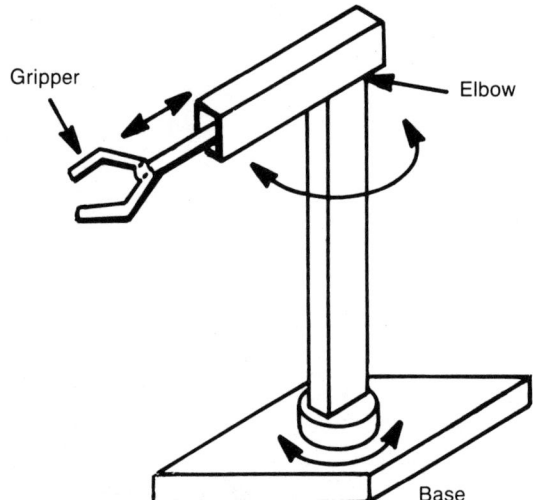

Fig. 8-3. *Spherical coordinate robot arm. This shows the main components and operation of a spherical coordinate arm.*

An *articulated* or *jointed spherical coordinate* arm has all the elements of the spherical arm; however, it also has elbow and wrist joints, allowing for greater flexibility of motion. Its ability to move in all directions makes it the most widely used of robot arms. See FIG. 8-4 for an illustration of this type of arm.

How Do Robots Work? 117

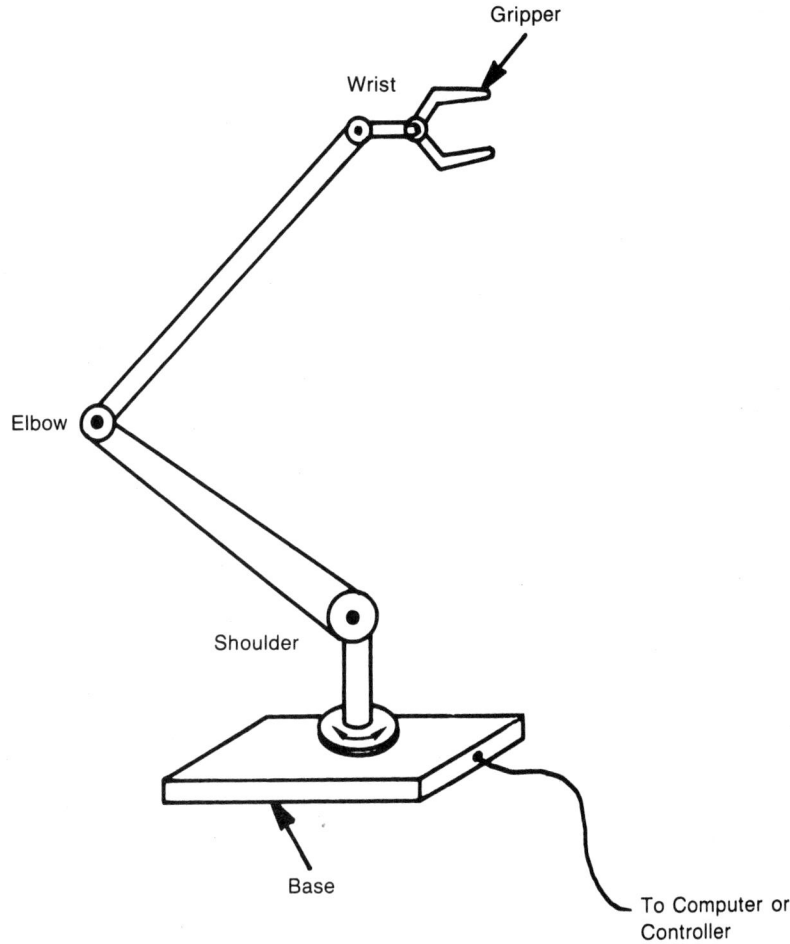

Fig. 8-4. *Articulated jointed spherical coordinate robot arm. This shows the components and operation of this type of robot arm.*

Finally, a *selective compliance robot assembly arm* (SCARA), is basically cylindrical in operating. It has a horizontally operated elbow joint that allows it to fold upon itself in either direction. This is useful for assembly applications. See FIG. 8-5 for an illustration of a SCARA arm.

End Effectors

On a robot arm, the arm does not do all of the work. The end effector does its part too, just as human hands do the work together with the

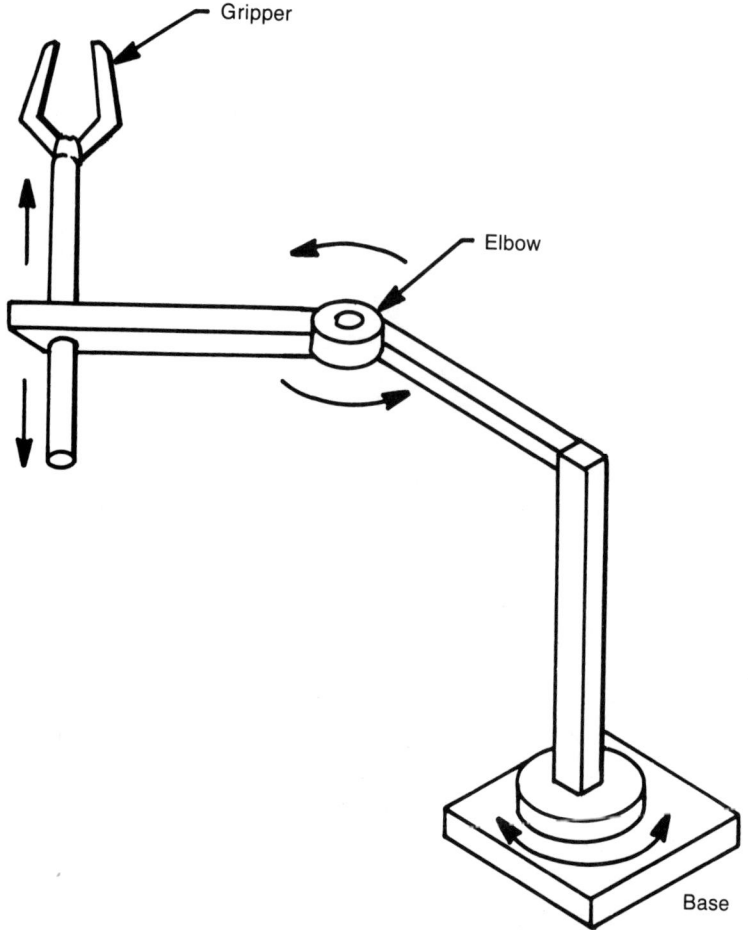

Fig. 8-5. SCARA robotic arm. This shows the major components of a SCARA (Selective Compliance Assembly Robot Arm), and how the arm operates.

arm. There are many different kinds of end effectors, but basically they are the part that handles the objects and performs operations upon some item. One of the most common forms of the end effector is the gripper. The simplest form has two "fingers" that can grasp and pick up items. For more sophisticated operations, three or more grippers can be used. The fingers of the gripper can be moved to accomplish the operations desired, and can rotate, swivel up and down, and back and forth. These motions give a robot assembly several more "degrees of freedom."

Actuators

Actuators are the power sources for robots, and can be either hydraulic, electric, or pneumatic. Hydraulic systems are very powerful and use a pressurized liquid such as oil or water under pressure. Heavy weights can be lifted using hydraulics.

Electric systems use motors to operate the movement of the arm, and work with gears and pulleys to create the movements. Finally, pneumatic systems use compressed air to effect movement of the arms and grippers.

Controllers

Controllers are the mechanisms that control the operation of the robot. Controllers send signals to the power source to move the robot arm to a certain position, and to move the end effector or gripper for a specific task. Controllers can be a set of electronic circuits specifically designed for use with that robot system, or a computer system that can send instructions to manipulate the arm and end effector in different ways, depending on the specific need.

There are different kinds of controllers, such as the open loop and servomechanism. The open loop is a type where no feedback is required from the arm; rather the controller moves it, making stops at certain points and then operating the end effector. Also known as a point-to-point system, it usually moves between two points and might pick up an object at point A and move it to B, then repeat the procedure. This is a rather simple method of controlling a robot.

A servo-controlled robot, on the other hand, uses feedback sensors to send information back to the controller or computer about the location of the arm and position of the joints. With this information as an analog voltage or numerical value, the controller can then complete the instructions to send the arm to the exact location desired. By designating the points and location desired, the arm can be controlled to the precise location desired and do very accurate work.

Teaching a robot how to do its job can be accomplished in one of two ways. The robot can be programmed on a point-to-point basis, designating the beginning, ending, and intermediate points desired. Alternately, a robot can be moved manually in various positions to simulate the desired actions, and the motions stored in memory as a sequence of signals. The stored sequence can be played back and the desired sequence run, without complex programming.

Robot Senses and Intelligence

Robots that can perform a fixed set of motions are fine; however, for them to do more sophisticated tasks, they need to have some kind of simulated senses: to "see" an electronic circuit board, to "feel" whether it is gripping an object too loosely or tightly, and "hearing" instructions in English.

Vision is an important sense for robots, that need to "see" what it is doing and determine whether a task has been done properly or not. By installing some video camera with the necessary equipment, it is possible to process and analyze images, and tie them into robot instructions.

Touch is important, because too loose or too tight a grip on a large slab of steel being moved can be the cause of disaster. Also, the robot should be able to detect whether or not it is actually touching an object. Various sensors to detect pressure, such as strain gauges and pressure transducers, can be used to determine what amount of pressure is being applied and compare it to what is needed for that particular object. A proximity detector will tell the robot how far an object is from the arm, using electrical signals.

Hearing is also a desirable sense, allowing robots not only to "hear" problems and unexpected noises, but also to "listen" to human commands in English, in other words, to communicate in natural language.

Smell and taste are also senses that can be developed. Smell, for instance, can be developed to detect fires, smoke, or noxious odors that might prove hazardous. Taste is probably not necessary, unless of course the technology progresses to the point where domestic robots are feasible.

Other senses, such as temperature, pressure, rate of flow, moisture, and speed can be useful if implemented in a computer.

Finally, robots can be made more "intelligent." Just like expert systems that are filled with in-depth information on a certain subject area, robots can be made more intelligent and fulfill many of the functions that we have imagined for many years. These include personal robots, domestic robots, instructional robots, and robots that can perform more "human" tasks. Making existing robots more intelligent is another goal that can be sought.

The future is bright, and robotics is one field where great practical use is a certainty. We can truly delegate many of our less pleasant, dangerous, and undesirable tasks to robots, who will work away continuously at our command.

Part III
Fifth-Generation Software and Applications

Chapter 9
Programming Languages

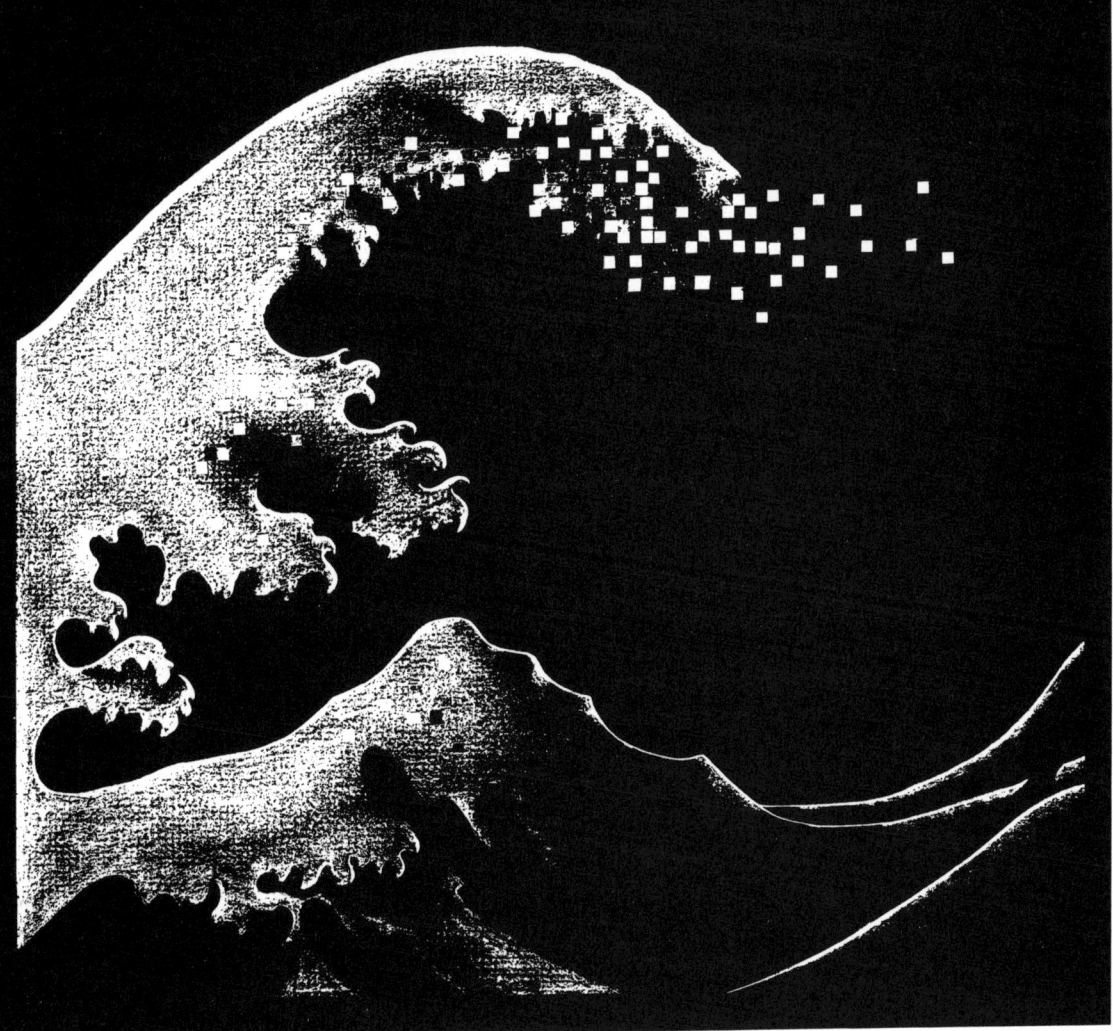

Creating software to work with all the new computers and other developments of the fifth generation requires a different class of programming languages than the ones used basically for education and data processing. The languages in use in business and industry, such as COBOL, FORTRAN, BASIC, and Pascal, often cannot be used effectively for the artificial intelligence applications being developed today.

Instead, special languages need to be used for fifth-generation applications. Of the two major languages being used for AI, one has been around for some time, while the other is relatively new. The two languages are LISP and PROLOG.

The purpose of this chapter is to introduce you to LISP and PROLOG, and to explore how they can be used for AI applications. Their special strengths and suitability for these kinds of uses also are discussed. Finally, a number of other, lesser-known languages are mentioned and described briefly.

LISP

LISP, an acronym for LISt Processor, is probably the most popular and widely used language for AI. LISP, which seems at once a forbidding mass of parentheses, is in actuality both simplistic and expressive. Its strength in representing data and dealing with lists makes it ideally suited for use in creating AI programs. Instead of dealing with data items (numbers, characters, etc.) as in a BASIC or Pascal program, information can be represented as symbols that are linked together in a specified relationship using lists. Various procedures and functions enable you to do a variety of operations on these lists and list structures.

Interestingly enough, LISP is one of the oldest programming languages still in existence. It was developed in the early 1950s by John

McCarthy, and the first commercial implementation was ready in the early part of the 1960s. This is just a few years behind the development of FORTRAN. Since this time, LISP has been developed and refined many times, and that is part of the reason why it has survived to the present.

The first version of LISP was designated as version 1.0. This eventually led to further revisions, such as LISP 1.5. A host of other versions and dialects that fall into four main varieties came out. MACLISP was developed at MIT and is quite well known. INTERLISP was created at Bolt, Bernandek, and Newman, and with MACLISP is implemented on special AI development computer systems known as LISP machines. Portable Standard LISP, developed at the University of Utah, is available on various systems; however, it did not become a standard, as it was hoped it would.

Common LISP was the result of a group of manufacturers and computer scientists who got together to attempt to designate some kind of standard LISP dialect. Strongly influenced by MACLISP, INTERLISP, and various other dialects, it has been predicted that Common LISP will make other earlier dialects obsolete.

LISP is an interpreted language, which means that each line is accepted, interpreted, and executed in a similar manner to a language such as BASIC. The language is available in a wide variety of versions and implementations, for computers from Apple IIs and IBMs all the way up to VAXes, IBM mainframes, and even special LISP machines.

The LISP language works in a different way from most languages. The basic unit of data in LISP is the atom. These ''words'' can be numbers or symbolic names for an object, place, or event. These atoms are then put together to form lists. You then manipulate these lists to achieve your desired result. Rather than statements or commands, you use procedures and functions to manipulate the data in the lists. Operations on lists are performed through procedure functions. They can be simple arithmetic functions, such as add, subtract, multiply, divide, or procedures that ask a question (predicates). Built-in procedures are known as primitives. In the following sections, you will see examples of how LISP really works, followed by some examples of LISP for AI applications.

Atoms and Lists: Building Blocks of LISP

Atoms are the most basic data element in LISP. An atom can be either a number (integer or real), or a symbol. Numbers can be in various forms and either negative or positive. Symbols are used to represent objects, whether people, places, things, or something else. Examples of atoms include 2.14, 7, BIRDS, GH79, or – .00005.

Lists, the major data structure in LISP, allow meaningful operations to be made on groups of atoms. Atoms, whether numbers or symbols, need to be assembled in some kind of meaningful order to be processed efficiently. A list is represented as a group of atoms contained within parentheses:

(ALABAMA ALASKA CALIFORNIA DELAWARE UTAH WYOMING)

The names of the states are the individual atoms or elements of the list, while the group as a whole is a list, perhaps named STATES. There is a single space that separates each element from the other. Also, as you will notice, there is usually some relationship between the elements as it exists. Lists need not consist entirely of atoms, but also can be made up of atoms and lists, or of other lists. For instance, the following is made up of a mixed set of atoms and lists:

(BILL (GEORGE JIM) DICK (JEFF DAVE MIKE) WILL)

while the following is made up entirely of other lists:

((AMY BETH JANE)(LISA MARY BETTY)(TAMMY RACHEL))

The use of multiple lists results in the use of many parentheses. The correct number of left and right parentheses must be maintained so that the code can be processed by LISP. A list, such as those shown here, can be referred to as expressions or S (symbolic) expressions. It is also possible to have an empty list, known as NIL or ( ).

Representation of Lists

While lists are represented using symbolic names and parentheses, the representation of the information inside the computer is quite different. In simplest terms, information is represented as a chain of CONS cells, which can be described as linked lists made up of two parts. Each contains an address, the first to where the actual data is stored, and the other to the next element in the list. A simple list would be a horizontal

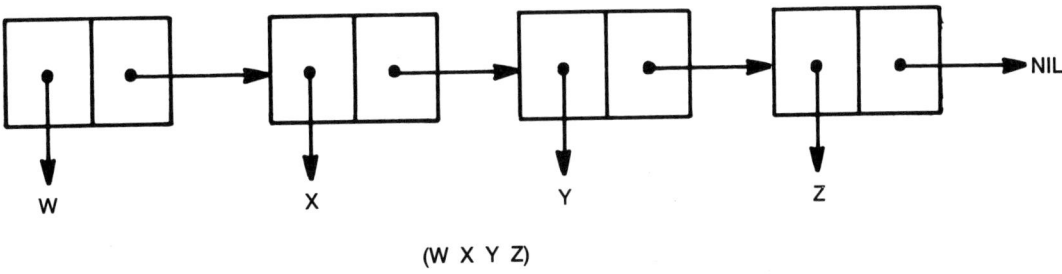

Fig. 9-1. *Internal representation of a list. This shows how elements of a LISP list are represented in memory. This is a simple list.*

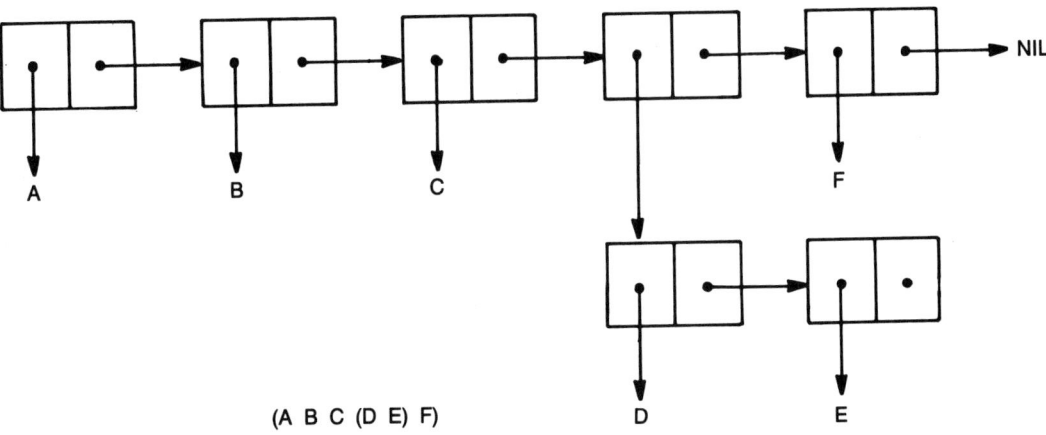

Fig. 9-2. *Internal representation of a complex list. This is a more involved example with one list located inside the other.*

chain of CONS cells, from beginning to end. A more complicated example, with one list within the other, is represented with two levels. See the examples of representations of two types of lists, FIGS. 9-1 and 9-2.

Procedures and Functions

A group of atoms or lists form what is known as a symbolic expression, or S expression. LISP is designed to operate on, evaluate, and produce output from these expressions, using procedures and functions. There is a fine difference between the two, but basically a procedure describes how data is to be processed, while a function computes a value based on various arguments that are given to it. While not all procedures are functions, all functions are procedures.

Built-in procedures that are provided by LISP are known as primitives, and can be used by simply specifying the name of the desired primitive. If you need to do something not covered by the primitives, you can define your own procedures and functions. In terms of primitives, the choices available to you will differ according to the computer, implementation, and dialect chosen. However, there is a set of basic primitives that is common to all dialects, and that will be covered here.

Arithmetic Primitives

The simplest primitives are those that perform computer arithmetic functions such as add, subtract, multiply, and divide. You will notice that the arrangement of the operator is unusual in that it appears first, and usually only two operators are allowed. Some dialects place the operator outside the parentheses, others inside. You can add two numbers as follows:

(+ 3 5)

which will return the result, 8.

To add more than two numbers, you need to use multiple lists, and keep somewhat of a running total:

(+ 3 (+ 5 (+ 7 5)))

which will add four numbers to produce the answer, 20.

Some dialects use English words in lieu of a mathematical operator, or offer a choice. Instead of using the + sign, for instance you could use the word PLUS:

(PLUS 33 66)

resulting in a total of 99.

The remaining primitive operators work in much the same way. There is the minus sign (-) for subtraction, or sometimes the command DIFFERENCE or DIF. Multiplication is usually represented by the asterisk (*), or by the command TIMES. For division, either the slash (/) or the primitive QUOTIENT is used. Dialects differ in their handling of integer and real number arithmetic as well. Naturally, with the proper manipulation of lists and operators, complex formulas can be created.

In addition to the simplest arithmetic, there are primitives that represent more complex functions, such as absolute value (ABS), exponentiation (EXPT), the largest and smallest numbers in a list (MAX and MIN), as well as square root (SQRT).

Predicates

Predicates are special procedures that answer questions posed to it about certain expressions with a "T" (TRUE) or "NIL" (FALSE) response. The determination of the answer is based on the value of the argument provided. To determine if an expression is a number, use NUMBERP:

(NUMBERP 5)

which returns T, while the following

(NUMBERP HIS)

would return NIL.

To find out if an expression is an atom, use ATOM:

(ATOM DOG)

which prints out T.

The same general idea holds for LISTP, which tests whether the expression is a list:

(LISTP DOG)

results in NIL, while the expression

(LISTP DOG CAT FROG)

returns T.

There are other predicates that work on several data items, and require an appropriate number of arguments. For instance, to determine if two items are the same, use EQUAL:

(EQUAL (A B) (A B))

which returns T.

As you can see, various predicates are useful for working with lists of atoms and numbers.

Most of the basic predicates work in the same general way, and following is a list of some of the major ones:

- NULL determines whether the list is empty.
- MEMBER determines whether the item described is a member of your list.
- MINUSP returns whether the item is negative.
- EVENP answers whether the item is even.
- GREATERP returns whether the first number in the list is greater than the second.
- LESSP returns whether the first number in the list is less than the second.

List Operations

In addition to arithmetic operations and predicates, list manipulation is an important part of LISP. By using these operations you can extract elements from a list, put together and take apart lists, and form new lists. There are several primitives that are available in most dialects of LISP:

CAR returns the first element in a list, as in the following example:

```
(CAR '(A B C D)
A
```

In this case, only the single element, "A," is returned. Using CAR on a group of lists gives a different result:

```
(CAR '((A B)(C D)(E F))
(A B)
```

CDR is the complement of the CAR function. In this case, everything except the first element or list is returned. CDR can be applied to a list of single elements:

```
(CDR '(A B C D))
(B C D)
```

or to a list of lists:

(CDR '((A B)(C D)(E F)))
((C D)(E F))

You might have noticed that a quote precedes each of the lists or parts of lists being worked on. The quote mark is a shorthand symbol for the function QUOTE that prevents each individual list or item from being evaluated. Instead, it tells LISP that you want to perform CAR or CDR on the entire set of data after the quote. This is known as quoting.

Another important list operation primitive is APPEND. This combines the elements of two lists to form a new, larger list, such as in the following example:

(APPEND '(A B C) '(D E F)))
(A B C D E F)

To add a new element to the front of an existing list, use CONS:

(CONS 'A '(B C D))
(A B C D)

or do this on a set of lists:

(CONS '(A B C) 'D E F)
((A B C)D E F)

The LIST primitive allows you to build new lists from separate elements or other lists. Here, you create a new list from single elements:

(LIST 'A 'B 'C)
(A B C)

or from two lists:

(LIST '(A B)(C D))
((A B)(C D))

Note the difference between the LIST and APPEND functions in relation to how they handle and create the new list.

Depending on the specific dialect you are working with, there might be other primitives for working with lists. However, the primitives discussed here are the most familiar and commonly used.

Assigning Values: SETQ

In many languages, you set the value of a variable using an operator such as = or := , in an expression such as A = 4 (assign 4 to A). In LISP there is a built-in primitive that accomplishes the same thing, known as SETQ. The function of this primitive is straightforward, such as

(SETQ A 4)

which sets the value of A to 4. After you assign this value, later commands will use A with the designated value of 4. For instance, the following will assign values to two variables and bring forth the sum:

(SETQ A 12)
(SETQ B 18)
(+ X Y)
30

Creating Your Own Functions

While a lot can be done using built-in functions, you will undoubtedly want to create functions that are more complex and solve the particular problem you are concerned with. The key to creating your own functions is through the use of the DEFUN (or other variant of this) function to combine various primitives into a meaningful new procedure or function. Similar to creating a subroutine in other languages, the process is known in more technical terms as *procedure abstraction*.

As an example, consider the classic case of the factorial, symbolized by N! You might recall that if you have 3!, then it equals $3*2*1 = 6$, finding the product of all numbers descending from N back to 1. By definition, 0! equals 1. This could be represented as a new function:

(DEFUN FACT(N)
    (COND ((ZEROP N) 1)
        (T (* N (FACT (- N 1SUB1))))))

This uses the concept of recursion, which will be discussed in a later section. However, you can get an idea of how a LISP function works.

Decision Making

Another important part of any language is its ability to evaluate various calculations and results and make decisions based on these values and conditions. These structures or statements are known as conditionals. In languages such as BASIC, IF..THEN structures are used to make decisions. In LISP, a primitive known as COND allows for decision making.

The general form of the COND primitive is as follows:

```
(COND (cond action))
      (cond 2 action 2)
      (cond 3 action 3)
          .
          .
          .
      (cond N action N))
```

In simplest terms, if the first (CONDition) part evaluates to true, then the corresponding action part will be evaluated (executed) and a result returned. A simple example could be shown in relation to grading a test on a pass/fail basis:

```
(DEFUN GRADE (SCORE)
(COND ( (GREATERP SCORE 59) 'PASS)
   ( (LESSP SCORE 60) 'FAIL) ) )
```

This simple function accepts a value for the score, and evaluates it, giving a grade. If the score is greater than 59, then it is a passing grade. Otherwise, if the score is less than 60, then the grade is a failing one.

Applications to Artificial Intelligence

The previous sections have given you a good idea of how LISP operates and how some of its many functions and procedures work. Because the topic of this book is the fifth generation and AI, it is best to take a look at how this language is applicable to AI and why researchers use LISP, rather than other languages for fifth generation work. Lists, rules, and frames are useful for knowledge representation, especially for work in the area of expert systems. Pattern matching and searching are two other general purpose AI applications that are widely used, and are also mentioned here.

Lists

LISP works with information in the form of lists, and lists are useful for AI work, because as an ordered sequence of objects, lists can be operated on as a whole with special primitives and functions. There is a special type of list that is especially useful for creating knowledge bases, known as a *property list*.

Property lists are created using the PUT or PUTPROP primitive, and there are four elements in the usual property list: the word PUTPROP, the atom or symbol you are creating, the name of the property, and the value of the property. Its general form could be written as follows:

(PUTPROP SYMBOL PROPNAME PROPVALUE)

with a more specific example as follows:

(PUTPROP GEORGE AGE 35)

which specifies that George is the symbol, the property is AGE, and the value of AGE is 35. Therefore, George is 35.

A property list is useful for representing knowledge in the form of a database, and with the use of various primitives, you can manipulate property lists.

Rules

A rule is an ideal way to represent heuristic knowledge in expert systems. The general form of any rule is IF..THEN where IF refers to the condition that needs to be satisfied and THEN refers to the action to take if the condition is true. One way to represent a rule is as follows:

```
(RULE name)
    (IF (condition)
        (condition2)
            and other conditions . . .
    (THEN (action) )
```

This general form gives a name to the rule, and then represents the information as IF..THEN statements. There can be multiple IF statements, all of which are considered to be ANDed together and related to the corresponding THEN statement. This structure shows how easily LISP can represent knowledge in a computer.

Frames

Frames also are related to expert systems, and they each contain "slots" that contain facts, information, and specifications about the certain symbol or object. Frames are closely related to property lists; however, frames are linked together in a hierarchical network structure, with lower-level frames inheriting the values of the high-level ones.

There is a data structure available in LISP that is ideal for implementing frames, known as association lists. This type of list consists of sublists, the first element of which is a *key* or *marker*, followed by various characteristics, properties, and values. The key tells you what is in the list, much like a keyword in database searching.

Using an association list to represent a frame is easy. You can set up this kind of list (also known as an A-list) as a FRAME, and designate various slots as sublists. Each slot is a list in itself, and can contain values of its own. Let's look at this in terms of LISP code:

(FRAME (SLOT A) (SLOT B) (SLOT C) . . . (SLOT Z))

is the general structure for the frame, and then each slot can be an A-list as well:

(SLOT A) (VALUE 1) (VALUE 2) (VALUE 3) . . .(VALUE N))

and at an even lower level, each "value" can have its own set of information as an A-list:

(VALUE 1 (IDEA 1) (IDEA 2) (IDEA 3) . . . (IDEA N))

Because A-lists are specific structures closely related to standard lists, you can use various primitives to search and retrieve information from any level of the frame structure.

Pattern Matching and Searching

Pattern matching and searching are widely used in AI applications, and can be implemented in LISP quite easily. For pattern matching, the predicate EQUAL is ideal, because it compares two symbols or lists and returns true (T) if they are identical and false (NIL) is they are not. Using EQUAL in a special function with COND and other primitives can produce a useful pattern procedure for your specific application.

Searching, which is usually done by searching through a network of nodes and arcs to find the desired information, is also easily done in LISP. The relationship between nodes can be specified through the use of sublists and nested lists, and property lists also can be used to specify not only the symbol but its relationship to the other elements. Using COND with an iterative or recursive technique is a good way to implement a searching procedure.

In summary, LISP is an unusual, yet easy-to-use and powerful language that is the one you should learn if you want to become involved in artificial intelligence. Its structure and operation is ideally suited to knowledge representation and other applications to AI. For many years, LISP was the only major AI language in use; however, another one has come along to challenge LISP's position. This language has attracted a following in the computer community, and was Japan's choice for work on its fifth-generation computer. The next section describes this bold new language, PROLOG.

PROLOG

While LISP is considered by many to be the premier AI language, other languages have gained a substantial following, and at the present time, the main competitor is PROLOG. PROLOG, short for PROgramming in LOGic, is quite a new language, and one which is based on an entirely new concept of programming.

PROLOG, invented in the early 1970s at the University of Aix-Marseille, is a descriptive and declarative language, rather than a procedural one. In other words, it does not deal with a certain sequence of steps or algorithm, but rather works with facts to try to deduce new information from them. The goal is to work with information from a problem-oriented rather than a solution-oriented point of view.

In simplest terms, programming in PROLOG is a totally different kind of experience from programming in other languages. You give the system a group or set of rules describing various symbols and objects and the relationships between them. Each of these statements is known as a clause, and you can ask questions, obtain new facts, and make deductions from the information given.

The PROLOG interpreter has a built-in inference engine that first allows you to state facts and relationships, and will search through the database you have created to produce new relationships and matches among data items.

Unlike conventional programming where you set up a certain step-by-step procedure, in PROLOG you set up a kind of database or knowledge base, and then query with various questions that ultimately will help you to solve the problem. The accuracy of the solution will depend in large part on the quality of the information in your database. The language is usually interpreted, although some compilers are available.

As should be obvious by now, PROLOG is ideally suited to the creation of expert systems, for natural language understanding, and for special applications such as math logic. Special features such as an inference engine, pattern matching, searching, and logical techniques are built in and do not need to be created as in other languages. The language is also easy to learn and is English-like, however it should be pointed out that it is not intended for general purpose use like BASIC or Pascal.

Programming in PROLOG involves three main steps:

- Declaring facts that describe objects and their relationships
- Declaring rules that describe the relationships between these objects
- Asking questions about these objects and the relationships between them

You can think of PROLOG programming as consisting of two parts: defining the database, and posing questions to PROLOG concerning the database. Also, unlike other languages, PROLOG does not have a strictly defined program structure. The closest description of its "structure" is that it is a list of facts making up the knowledge or database.

Putting Facts into the Database

Creating a PROLOG database is somewhat like building a miniature expert system. In PROLOG, to create a database you enter various facts and relationships. Depending on the specific interpreter and statements used, you can enter facts in a form such as

owns (Andy, IBM-PC).

owns (Connie, Compaq).

owns (Adrienne, Apple Mac II).

or in an alternate form (Micro-Prolog SIMPLE) as:

(Andy husband-of Connie)

(Connie wife-of Andy)

(Andy father-of Adrienne)

(Connie mother-of Adrienne)

(Adrienne daughter-of Andy)

(Adrienne daughter-of Connie)

Another type of clause can have only one argument:

black (Compaq)

meaning that "The Compaq is black." In fact, all of the relationships previously listed can be represented in words, because the relationships are all clear and straightforward. The previous clause can be represented alternately as:

color (Compaq, black)

which says much the same thing.

Asking Questions

Even with the simple database specified in the two formats just outlined, you can begin asking questions and obtain answers from PROLOG's inference engine. You can ask a question such as

owns (Adrienne, Apple Mac II)?
Yes

which confirms the fact that Adrienne owns an Apple Mac II. However, if you ask another question:

? owns (Adrienne, Compaq).
No

the answer is No. In this case, the question is asked in a different format, but the result is the same. The syntax would vary between dialects.

Of course, if the responses were limited to only yes and no responses, PROLOG would be much like an electronic version of "20 Questions." However, you also can use variables to ask PROLOG to respond with elements from the database, such as the following:

owns (Connie, X)?
X = Compaq

which asks what Connie owns. The answer? Compaq.

Conjunctions

In the previous examples, you only matched up one condition before returning an answer. It is also possible to match two different conditions using an "and"-type conjunction. In this case, you specify two different conditions and PROLOG will search for the applicable result, if any:

owns (Connie,X), color(X, black)?
X = Compaq

Here, two conditions, owned by Connie and is black must be satisfied.

Information represented in these examples is known as fact, and is one way to put information into PROLOG. Another way is in the form of rules. Rules consist of an IF part and a THEN part. IF the condition is met, THEN the action is taken.

The following is an example of a rule:

IF X is a man (male)
AND X is a parent of Y
THEN X is the father of Y

and this is how it can be implemented in PROLOG:

```
father_of (X,Y) :
male (X),
parent (X,Y).
```

By studying this example, you can see how PROLOG represents this information—THEN portion first—followed by the various conditions. Through a collection of these rules, you can create a database of rules and ask questions concerning the information and relationships.

Mathematical Operations

PROLOG has a set of mathematical operators that can do the standard functions of addition, multiplication, division, subtraction, as well as make comparisons of equal to, greater than, less than, and various combinations. These usually are used in conjunction with the PROLOG techniques previously described. Because PROLOG is not strong in the area of mathematics—and these commands are covered quite well in books on the language—consult language books for more information on the syntax and details of mathematical operations. Also, keep in mind that the coverage of PROLOG in this section is brief and introductory—more complex logic and commands are not described here. The best approach is to consult a PROLOG programming book to obtain further details on how to program in PROLOG.

In summary, PROLOG is a logical, descriptive programming language that is much like an expert system with an empty knowledge base. By programming, you fill in this knowledge base and create a database of knowledge on a certain subject. You then use the language's built-in inference engine to ask questions and attempt to find an answer. Without a doubt, PROLOG is ideal for use in various AI needs, and is an "up and coming" language that together with LISP will give you great power and versatility.

Other Languages

LOGO is commonly associated with graphics, turtles, and children's educational programming. Although one of the purposes of the language is to simplify the teaching of computer concepts and programming to young students, it also is a powerful programming language that can be used to create AI applications. LOGO is considered a close relative of the LISP language, and is available on various personal computers.

Smalltalk is a language based on a different approach from conventional languages such as LISP and PROLOG. Smalltalk is an object-oriented language based on an earlier language known as Simula. The subject of Smalltalk is the object (or actor) that is a data item either numerical or symbolic. This object is operated on by sending messages between objects, with the message representing a word describing an operation that can be performed on the object. When the object receives the message, it carries it out on itself and returns a response. The details of how all this works is complex, so consult a book on Smalltalk if you desire more information. Also, Digitalk has a version available for the IBM PC.

Stanford Artificial Intelligence Language (SAIL) is a descendent of Algol, a language developed in the 1960s. The focus of Algol, and subsequently, SAIL, is on developing algorithms and using them on a variety of computers. SAIL has the feature of being able to construct a database using "triples," which can be searched using pattern matching techniques. Consult a SAIL text for more information.

PLANNER is a language based on the principle of a database made up of theorems and assertions. This database can be searched using search and pattern techniques. PLANNER can be written in LISP.

CONNIVER is a variant of PLANNER, and is more powerful because it has more control structures to control and augment the search process.

POPLER is similar to CONNIVER and PLANNER; however it is written in POP-2, a language with the combined strengths of LISP and Algol.

AMORD is related to POPLER, CONNIVER, and PLANNER and is quite similar in structure and capabilities.

OPS5 is a language that focuses on rules, and uses production rules to represent knowledge. Its main purpose is for producing expert systems, and has a forward-chaining inference engine. OPS5 is not merely an expert system shell or tool, but is a full language that really takes advantage of the use of rule structures. OPS5 is available for IBM PC and Macintosh computers.

LOOPS and FLAVORS are two other object-oriented languages closely related to Smalltalk. LOOPS also has procedure, data, and rule-oriented programming. FLAVORS is a language related to Smalltalk that was designed to run on various LISP machines.

FRL and KRL are frame-based languages. Frame Representation Language (FRL) uses the common form of frames with slots and inheritance.

Knowledge Representation Language (KRL) is closely related to both FRL and LOOPS. FRL and LOOPS are written in LISP.

In Summary

Programming languages abound, whether they be the major ones such as LISP and PROLOG, or one of the multitude of lesser-known ones. These languages are being used to create the software that will run the new generation of computer systems and control the new technologies of the fifth generation. Whatever your interest, knowing these languages will give you practical skills for expanding the frontiers of knowledge in computers and AI.

Chapter 10
Natural Language

Since the dawn of the computer age 40 years ago, making computers that can converse and work with "natural languages"—such as English—has changed from a dream to an obsession. The advantages of having such linguistically competent machines is obvious, from user friendly computer programs to automatic machine translation.

At first glance, natural language seems relatively easy compared to other tasks computers can do, such as play chess. But even the most technically advanced supercomputers today cannot even approach the natural language capabilities of an average five-year old. As researchers soon found, natural language does not pertain to computers as much as it does to all linguistically related fields such as philosophy, linguistics, and psychology.

Indeed, in 1949, the idea of "natural language" did not appear to pose a great problem. Computers were still new and already had been used extensively during World War II to break enemy codes successfully. Warren Weaver, then director of natural science for the Rockefeller Foundation, outlined a proposal in his paper, *Translation*, for "the solution of worldwide translation problems." After all, if computers could already break codes during the war, what could be so different about language? According to Weaver, languages were just codes too. To him, an article in another language "is really written in English, but it has been coded in some strange symbols." It was a straightforward approach. Weaver called for an automatic translation machine, programmed with a bilingual dictionary. To "decode," the machine would simply substitute each word of the language to be translated with its equivalent in the other language (FIG. 10-1). Then this string of words could just be rearranged to fit their proper grammatical word order according to the then current theories of language structure. Of course, idioms and words in context would have to be taken into account and programmed into

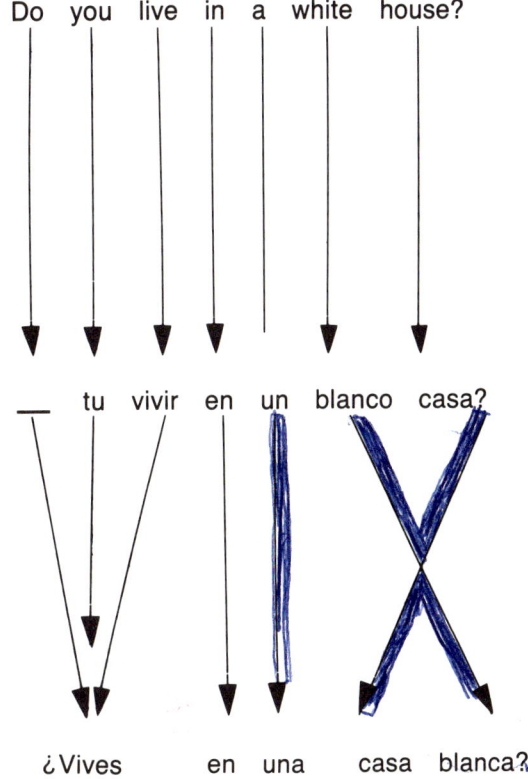

Fig. 10-1. *The basic idea behind machine translation. When efforts began in the 1950s, the process was thought to be little more than a glorified dictionary, which would translate a sentence into its other language equivalent word for word, and then simply rearrange and alter the translated vocabulary in order for it to make grammatical sense.*

the machine. On the surface, it looked as if it was just a technical problem of vocabulary and storage.

Worldwide, the natural language field exploded to the task. Research was funded, conferences held, and programs made. Scientists hurriedly tested new ideas. By 1954, a new journal, *Machine Translation* (MT), had been founded, and the first fruits of natural language research were appearing, riding a crest of publicity and anticipation. But these first attempts were little more than glorified dictionaries, and yielded translations that were all but impossible to understand, little better than the "codes" they were designed to replace. By 1966, only minute progress had been made in improving the quality of these programs, and the natural language field crept along at a turtle's pace. By the end of the year, the National Research Council's Automatic Language Processing Advisory Committee recommended that most funding for machine translation research be stopped.

The early accounts of these initial stabs at natural language have become embedded in the folklore of computer history. As one popular legend goes, computer researchers were once trying out a new machine translation program, translating English to Russian and back to English again. When they asked the computer to translate "The spirit is willing, but the flesh is weak" the English translation they got in return said, "The vodka is good but the meat is rotten."

It became clear from these efforts that machine translation programs could not just look at a sentence's words and structure, but would have to "understand" what these words meant and be able to analyze their relationships. One Israeli researcher, Yehoshua Bar-Hillel noted, "A translation machine should not only be supplied with a dictionary but a universal encyclopedia."

Natural Language Understanding

Natural language understanding programs today are usually divided into several major components, each corresponding to a different level of analysis. These include morphology, lexicon, syntax, semantics, and pragmatics. Morphology deals with the basic rules of spelling and words, decomposing sentences into their empirical word roots and verb forms. Lexical analysis references this output in a dictionary, identifying words as nouns and verbs and attaching this information to the sentence. Syntactic analysis takes this information and determines the structure of the sentence, separating it into its constituent parts so that semantic analysis can translate this syntactic form into an internal representation of its meaning. Finally, pragmatic analysis takes each sentence in context, considering the intent of each speaker according to setting, time, and the matter being discussed.

Syntax

Morphological and lexical analysis perform basic steps of the natural language understanding process and do not require very computationally difficult programming to accomplish. However, over the past

30 years, a great deal of debate has ensued in theoretical linguistics over the best approaches to syntactical analysis.

Conventionally known as *parsing*, syntactical analysis breaks up sentences into their component parts. Literally thousands of different parsers have been written for specific tasks. Some need intensive knowledge of the meaning of a particular sentence. Others need comply only with simple English commands.

One of the frontrunners of this pack is the Augmented Transition Network, first developed in the early 1970s by William Woods at Bolt, Beranek, and Newman in Cambridge, Massachusetts, and still considered as the state-of-the-art parser of its kind. The Augmented Transition Network, or ATN, tests each word in the sentence and its grammatical relation with the other words encountered previously, and tries to find what role the word plays in the sentence as a whole. The ATN performs this task by using a series of rules, such as the rules of grammar, which are applied to the sentence to determine its structure. This kind of parsing is called *context-free* parsing, because it deals with the possible structures of a sentence without employing any knowledge of the sentence involved. Thus in context-free parsing, *The car showered with orange juice* is grammatically correct, although semantically it is meaningless.

The ATN is a *transitional* parser, meaning that it deals with the grammatical transitions between parts of speech. For example, a noun phrase might be *The ugly boy over there*. What the ATN does is break down this noun phrase into is parts—the noun phrase *The ugly boy* and the prepositional phrase *over there*. Delving even deeper, *The ugly boy* can be dissected further, into the article *the*, the adjective *ugly*, and finally the noun *boy*.

What the ATN consists of is a network of *machines* and *states*. Each machine represents a grammatical rule, such as Sentence = Noun Phrase + Verb Phrase. In this case, there are three states: S3, or state 3, is the sentence, S1 is the noun phrase, and S2 is the verb phrase. These three states are "linked" together in a series, S1-S2-S3. To have a grammatically correct sentence, the ATN must make the "transition" between S1 and S3 by fulfilling the requirements of S1 and S2. In other words, to make a grammatically correct sentence, you must have a noun phrase and a verb phrase. S1, or noun phrase, can consist of the rule Noun Phrase = Adjective (+) Noun (+) Prepositional Phrase. For S1 to be true, each of its states—S4, adjective; S5, noun; and S6, prepositional

148 Natural Language

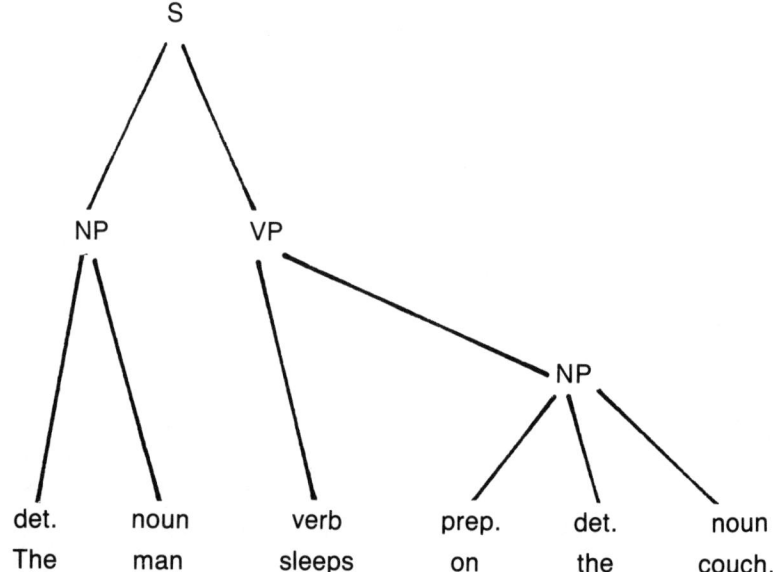

Fig. 10-2. A sentence "diagram." Before a computer can start any analysis as to what a sentence means, it must first be able to identify if an input sentence is grammatical or not. Here, a typical sentence is dissected into its constituent parts, a noun predicate and a verb predicate containing another noun predicate.

phrase—must be completed. For the prepositional phrase to be completed, its rule Prepositional Phrase = Preposition + Noun Phrase also must be satisfied, and so on and so on down. In this way, the ATN builds up a network of grammar that is very good at discovering the syntactical structure of any given sentence (FIG. 10-2).

While existing grammars and parsers can deal with 90% of all sentences, no matter how powerful a system is, there are still sentences it cannot handle. Despite these small shortcomings, syntactic analysis remains the best understood aspect of natural language processing.

Ambiguity is considered one of the major stumbling blocks of natural language research today. Any given sentence can have a plethora of possible syntactic structures. Take the sentence *He saw that gasoline can explode*. There are two different points of view for this sentence. Is the gasoline able to explode? Or is the gasoline container exploding? In this case, *He saw that gasoline can explode* is an example of structural ambiguity.

Fig. 10-3. Ambiguity. The pitfall of natural language understanding is ambiguity. Not only can words have several meanings, such as "page," which might refer to a person or to a piece of paper, words can have confusing pronoun references and grammatical structures, which cause natural language programs to stumble.

> I could not find the page.
> **page** n 1. A boy employed to run errands, carry messages or guide people.
> **page** n 2. One side of a leaf, as of a book, letter, newspaper or manuscript.

Lexical ambiguity, the most common form of ambiguity, occurs when a single word has more than one possible meaning. *I could not find the page* might refer to part of a text or to an attendant (FIG. 10-3). In most cases, the solution to ambiguous sentences is obvious within context to a human reader because they understand the sentence situation and can pick out the meaning that makes the most sense. Some programs attempt to use statistics to choose which meaning is more appropriate, which yields the correct choice in many cases, but also the wrong one in many others.

Deep structure refers to the basic meaning of a sentence. In deep structure ambiguity, two possible meanings might result from the same syntactic structure, such as in the sentence *The chickens are ready to eat*. Both interpretations refers to eating, but as to who or what is unclear.

Another type of ambiguity—semantic—results if a phrase in a sentence can be understood as having more than one meaning. Take the sentence *Joe wants to marry a Japanese*. Is *Japanese* a specific person that Joe wants to marry, or is it referring to a general class of people?

In pragmatic ambiguity, pronouns and special nouns such as "one" and "another" might refer to one of several objects in a sentence. A simple sentence involving pragmatic ambiguity is *Bill fought Mike because he loved Mary*. Who loved Mary is unclear.

Realizing the shortcomings of traditional syntactic parsing, linguist Charles Fillmore in 1968 wrote a treatise called *The Case for Case*, which argued the fact that more knowledge is essential for more natural language understanding. He proposed a parser that would look at the role, or case, each word had in a sentence. A sentence such as *John gave Mary a penny* would have three major cases: *John*, the agent: *Mary*, the recipient; and *penny*, the object. Each verb in a sentence would also be linked to cases that it required in a sentence, stored in a *frame* containing pertinent facts about each verb. The frame for the verb break might look like *agent, object, instrument*. In a system, there might be anywhere from 6 to 30 different types of cases, ranging from the fundamental *agent, counteragent* and *object* to the more specialized *instrument, goal,* and *experiencer*. Thus if given an input such as *Joe hit Bob with the stick*, the computer would be able to answer queries such as *What was Bob hit with?* by looking up the appropriate case, *instrument* in this example. It would then be able to answer simply, *the stick*.

One example of Fillmore's case grammar is Lexical Functional Grammar (LFG), developed by Ronald Kaplan and Joan Bresnan at the Xerox Palo Alto Research Center (PARC). Exactly as Fillmore proposed, LFG examines the functional roles of the words in a sentence, yielding a much more intuitive representation of language that is still expressed mathematically. The Japanese Fifth Generation Project has chosen LFG as its parser for its Natural Language Processing research.

Looking at sentences as functions and expressions rather than rigid grammatical structures is a prevalent attitude in AI research today. Parsers over the past few years have concentrated on the role and relationship of words in a sentence. These functional grammars, also called nontransitional grammars, point out the interdependence of syntax and semantics and act as a bridge between them.

Semantics

Elaine Rich, author of *Artificial Intelligence*, once noted, "Producing a syntactic parse of a sentence is only the first step toward understanding that sentence. At some point, a semantic interpretation of the sentence must be produced." But how can this be done? How can a computer really "understand" a phrase?

The key to semantics is a good representation of the information to be manipulated. While predicate calculus might be a fine representation for theorem proving, it might not be efficient for a machine translation program. Semantics is knowledge. But in a broader sense, it is ultimately everything.

One of the major pioneers of semantic research is Roger Schank of Yale University. During the early 1970s, he developed a model of *conceptual dependency* based on a conviction that sentences were only elaborate data structures built around a relatively small general concept. What Schank did was to narrow down and classify all these possible concepts into what he called *semantic primitives*. Each primitive is representative of an entire class of similar actions or ideas. For example, the single primitive PTRANS stands for all verbs such as *lift*, *walk* or *move*, which are related to changing the physical location of an object. The primitive STATE refers to verbs such as *death*, and so on. There are five primitives for physical acts: PROPEL, MOVE, INGEST, EXPEL, AND GRASP. There are three primitives for mental acts: CONC, MTRANS, and MBUILD; and two for instrumental acts: ATTEND and SPEAK. Finally, two primitives for global acts: PTRANS and ATRANS. Of course a number more can be created as necessary.

The result of primitives is a concise way of categorizing knowledge about the relationships of objects in a sentence into a formalism that is compact, if not well organized. Not surprisingly, semantic primitives easily can paraphrase sentences, which is at least an important step toward machine translation. Indeed, one of the goals of Schank's work was to make such implicit ideas explicit.

MARGIE, (meaning, analysis, response generation, and inference in English) developed during the early 1970s by Schank at the Stanford AI lab, was part of his early attempt to test his theory of conceptual dependency. MARGIE simply analyzed sample text, but "it was the first time a system could paraphrase, translate, and draw inferences from English sentences." If given a sentence such as *John sold an apple to Mary for 25 cents*, it would create an internal representation of the relationships involved. This sentence involves two actions, John giving Mary an apple and Mary giving John 25 cents. MARGIE would identify both as transfers, and use the appropriate semantic primitive ATRANS. In a method reminiscent of Fillmore's case grammar, MARGIE would create a "frame" for the sentence:

ATRANS: relation: owner < - > ATRANS: relation: owner
actor: John < - >   actor: Mary
object: apple < - >   object: 25 cents
source: John < - >   source: Mary
recipient: Mary < - >recipient: John

The arrows between the two primitives indicate a pair of primitives as part of a single expression.

By representing sentences in this fashion, if the program encounters a PTRANS verb within a sentence, it knows that it involves the changing of a physical location of an object and expects to find an object elsewhere in the sentence. This is useful in understanding incomplete or ambiguous information, and gives the program a deeper understanding of the text.

Also, by relying on a frame representation, conceptually equivalent sentences such as *Frank was phoned by Susan* and *Susan gave Frank a call* are represented similarly.

Following this approach, the obvious solution to natural language understanding is more knowledge. Every sentence occurs in a setting, and its particular meaning is related to the situation, speakers, and subject at that particular moment. What pragmatics does is use this contextual knowledge to analyze sentences and understand them.

Pragmatics

Pragmatic analysis usually is the last step in a typical natural language understanding program, and deals with most of the implied facts that are not specifically stated in a sentence. Almost as a rule, pragmatic analysis must contain a broad range of general knowledge about the world to be able to identify and recognize most contexts.

If a typical person asks someone "Can you pass the salt?" or "Do you know what time it is?", replying "Yes" would be annoying. ("Yes, I can pass the salt." Yes, I know what time it is.") Pragmatics tells us that the most *appropriate* response would be to give the salt to the speaker or to tell someone the time.

What the computer must do is distinguish between the literal meaning of language and the presupposed ideas behind them. The strange thing is, as computer science and AI researchers begin to explore pragmatics, they are finding themselves scratching the surface of applied philosophy and psychology.

Roger Schank and his colleagues at Yale have taken the straightforward approach to pragmatics: more general knowledge. They have extended their ideas on primitives and have taken them one step further, developing a concept of *scripts* outlining the series of events and relationships of objects and actions in particular situations.

The name script is very appropriate. These scripts encode knowledge of the real world in a form that the program can make inferences from. They might list for example, the sequence of typical events of eating a meal at a restaurant. The script might look like:

```
EAT-AT-RESTAURANT:        event-sequence:
props                     first look menu
roles                     then order meal
point of view             then eat meal
time of occurrence        then pay bill
place of occurrence       finally leave restaurant
```

From his ideas on scripts, in 1975 Schank created Script Applier Mechanism (SAM), a program that read, summarized, and answered queries about newspaper reports on auto accidents. If given say, the script in the example and the sentence *Vincent went to a restaurant and ordered a steak*, the computer would be able to infer from its script that Vincent also ate his steak and paid for it. To its advantage, SAM could infer things on a larger scale than what was provided for in the sentence.

SAM works as long as it deals with events called for in its scripts. But how does it account for unique situations?

Schank's work is part of a view of language understanding known as a *top down* process, and those words serve as cues for retrieving expectations from memory. A person uses these expectations to then make plans and goals, for and against established expectations. Previous research had concentrated on language as a *bottom up* process, where the meaning of individual words translated into the meaning of phrases and finally the meaning of the sentence.

Schank embodied his ideas in Plan Applier Mechanism (PAM), a new system he created in 1976 to read and interpret brief stories. (A sample PAM dialogue is in FIG. 10-4.) If given the sentences *John wanted to go to a movie. He walked to the bus stop*, and the going-to-the-movie script was not in its system, it would identify John's goal as *to go somewhere* and attempt to find a plan to accomplish that goal. According to its knowledge of going somewhere, John might have the available options of riding an animal, driving a car, walking, or public transportation. It would then identify the bus stop and its relation to public transportation and infer that *John took a bus to go to the movie*.

PAM also identified themes, such as love and betrayal, which symbolized interactions between two parties. PAM could take sentences such as *John loves Mary. Mary was stolen by a dragon*, and correctly locate a theme: love, and infer that its goal was *to rescue Mary from the dragon*. It would then develop a plan to fulfill that goal. If plans worked so well together that they became routine, they would be stored as scripts. In this way, PAM would be able to "learn" information about the outside world.

Summary

Many commercial natural language interfaces have already appeared on the market, and it appears that natural language is finally coming

PAM (1976)

Processing Paragraph 1:
   Richard hadn't heard from his college roommate Paul for years. Richard had borrowed money from Paul which was never paid back. But now he had no idea where to find his old friend. When a letter finally arrived from San Francisco, Richard was anxious to find out how Paul was.

USER: Who is Paul?
PAM: Richard's friend.
USER: Did Richard want to see Paul?
PAM: Yes, Richard wanted to know how Paul was.
USER: Had Paul lent money to Richard.
PAM: Yes, Paul lent money to Richard.
USER: Why didn't Richard pay Paul back?
PAM: Richard did not know where Paul was.
USER: How did Richard feel when the letter appeared?
PAM: Richard felt glad because Paul and he were friends.

Fig. 10-4. *A conversation with PAM. Built in 1976 by Roger Schank of Yale, PAM uses its knowledge of plans and goals to interpret brief stories and answer questions.*

of age. People are discovering the increased performance and productivity gains of using natural language interfaces.

While most of the uses for natural language in the past have been for database or as front ends, some of the new applications of natural language include *content scanning*: using a natural language system to scan through messages and load them into a standard format, and *text editing*: employing natural language's syntactical capabilities to correct style and grammar in written language.

While natural language understanding is still in its infancy, forecasts for natural language are sunny. The limited power and capabilities of contemporary computing make it impossible to predict where natural language research will lead. But with projected sales of natural language related products expected to top $1.5 billion by 1995, there is no question that natural language processing will open up bigger horizons for a whole new class of users.

Chapter 11
Expert Systems

You are rushed into the emergency room and are faced by grim-looking nurses. They stare at you with a combination of concern and exhaustion. You are afraid, not knowing what the prognosis will be. You look around for a doctor, but there are none to be found. You are growing more concerned, not sure why they are not calling a doctor or doing something. The only equipment in sight is a computer terminal, its cursor blinking in anticipation.

Finally, although you are in a weakened state and can hardly stay conscious, a stern, gray-haired nurse approaches your bedside and starts asking questions.

You answer, trying to give coherent responses. The nurse starts typing into the terminal and continues the interrogation amid taps to the keyboard. You finally manage one question:

"What's that?" you mutter.
"MYCIN," she responds, "and it'll tell me what's the matter with you."
"Where's the doctor?" you continue.
"What doctor?"

While it is unlikely that you'll be diagnosed entirely by computer in the near future, expert systems are playing an increasingly important role in a surprisingly large number of fields and professions, including agriculture, chemistry, computers and electronics, geology, law, math, engineering, the military, and of course medicine. Expert systems can be very useful in providing the necessary knowledge for solving problems, both with other experts and by itself.

What exactly is an *expert system*? Simply put, it is a special-purpose computer program that contains a great deal of specific, detailed knowledge about a certain problem area. This is an "intelligent" program that derives its intelligence from the vast amount of information it holds. Instead of just programming an algorithm or procedure, knowledge engineers work with human experts in the field to create systems that simulate the strategies, procedures, knowledge, and rules of thumb of a trained doctor, scientist, or other professional.

In a sense, expert systems transfer the information found in a human expert into a computerized form, making it able to solve problems in a certain specialized area in much the same way that a trained professional would.

What are the features of expert systems? First, the main "heart" of any expert system is its core of organized, specialized information, which makes the program "intelligent." Then, there is the expertise for problem solving that is unique to expert systems. This expertise will often include that of top experts in the field, making an expert system's solutions accurate, appropriate, and efficient. This skill and expertise makes expert systems commercially valuable and useful.

Expert systems also can do predictive modeling, providing answers for various problem solutions, testing out various options, and evaluating new approaches and strategies. Also, expert systems can be made to "remember" policies, opinions, previous strategies used, and other key information that can be used for further study and analyses.

Finally, expert systems can be used for training, because they have a strong body of knowledge from which to work, and can use the accumulated information and experience to offer detailed and efficient instruction.

Why Use Expert Systems?

A good question could be raised: why use expert systems? There are certainly many human experts available, and it seems that all the effort put into developing expert systems is unnecessary. However, there are some very good reasons why expert systems are valuable and worth the time and expense to create.

To start, there are many limitations to human experts. Human expertise is perishable, and knowledge that is not used by a person quickly fades. Second, transfer of knowledge from a human to another source is a laborious and inefficient process (commonly known as education, or in the case of expert systems, knowledge engineering), while artificial expertise easily can be transferred by coping or transmitting a program or set of data.

Documentation of human knowledge also is difficult, while recording how knowledge is represented in a computer is simple and straightforward. Also, while humans are inconsistent and at times unreliable and inaccurate, artificial means is almost always consistent and reliable. The reason for this is while both humans and machines can possess the same amount and type of knowledge, humans are subject to the effects of stress, memory lapse, emotional trauma, and the normal variations in emotional state common to people.

A final factor that makes expert systems attractive is cost. Human experts, especially the highly trained top-notch experts, are scarce and expensive. They are in demand and receive high salaries. While expert systems are difficult and expensive to create, after completion the system can be run very inexpensively for a minimum of operating and maintenance cost.

All these factors make expert systems seem like the perfect answer to all our modern needs for knowledge and expertise; however, there is a negative side to artificial expertise.

First, expert systems are not creative. They cannot solve problems using new approaches and methods. Rather, they simply use the information they are given to draw conclusions and provide output. Creativity and "brainstorming" for new approaches is not part of an expert system's strength.

Closely related to this is the fact that expert systems do not learn quickly. While they can be made to implement new information and methods, they cannot adjust to new situations and conditions and learn from them. Any "learning" program that is available now is still quite limited in its power and usefulness.

Also, humans can use a variety of sensory input—sight, sound, touch, smell, and others—to analyze and solve problems. Computers, on the other hand, can only manipulate symbols, and often the direct meaning of something is "lost in the translation." In addition, people can look at a problem from both the narrow and the broad focus, while computers can take only the focus in which it has been designed. The reason for this is because it takes a great deal of expertise and work to handle the main problem by itself, and even more to handle the many hundreds of associated problems that would form the "big picture."

However, this problem is expected to be solved, with greater experience in creating expert systems.

Finally, people have a large store of what could be termed general or "common-sense" knowledge that can eliminate an inappropriate alternative or result right away. A machine would need to have an enormous knowledge base to encompass the wide range of information that constitutes general knowledge.

So, with these two factors in mind, expert systems have been delegated to the role of an "advisor" that works in conjunction with an expert or even a novice user in the subject area.

Structure of Expert Systems

Now that you have some idea of what expert systems are all about, and what their strengths and limitations are, we can begin to look at the structure of expert systems. This involves not only how the information itself is represented within the knowledge base, but how the entire system is put together, knowledge base, inference engine, and all.

First of all, information is represented using one of several methods: facts, rules, frames, and semantic nets. While these concepts will be discussed in a following section, it would suffice to say that information is represented in various ways, including IF . . . THEN statements, data structures consisting of "slots" for information, and a hierarchical network of nodes that shows the logical relationship of various pieces of information. Much of this information is heuristic rather than algorithmic. In other words, the information contains rules of thumb, strategies, and simplifications that make it easier to find solutions when a problem is complex or not well understood. This is in contrast to a purely algorithmic approach where there is a specific formula to use to reach a solution.

The rules, facts, frames, and semantic nets make up what is known as the domain knowledge or knowledge base. However, information by itself is not enough to make for an efficient expert system. There is a second major component to expert systems, and this is known as the inference engine. The inference engine is a most important part of the entire system, because for the system to be of any use, there must be knowledge about how to make effective use of the information contained within the knowledge base. In order words, the knowledge base contains the organized information, while the "inference engine" has the

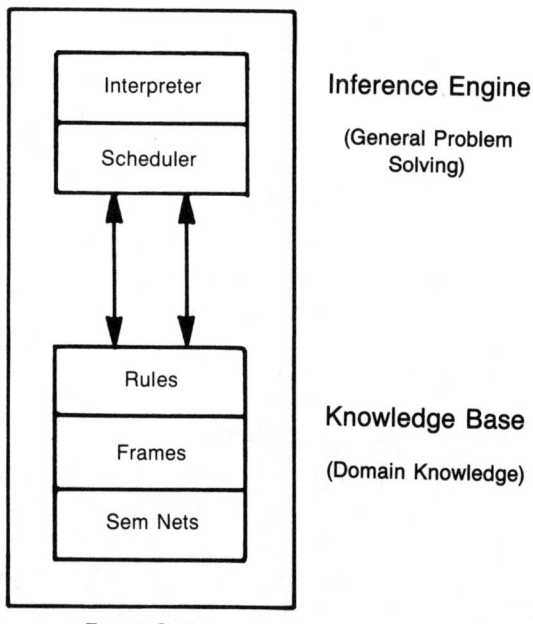

Fig. 11-1. Basic parts of an expert system. This shows the main parts of an expert system, including the inference engine and knowledge base.

general problem-solving knowledge for manipulating and using the stored expertise. See FIG. 11-1 for a diagram of an expert system.

What Tasks Can Expert Systems Perform?

In the broadest sense, expert systems deal with knowledge, while standard programs deal with data. MYCIN works with specialized knowledge on bacterial infections, diagnosing infections, and suggesting treatments. PROSPECTOR is an expert in helping geologists find ore deposits. On the other hand, a typical COBOL program, for example, would take payroll data, manipulate it, and create reports for businesses.

Expert systems typically offer the benefits of expertise, symbolic reasoning, depth, and knowledge about itself. They are usually skillful at producing solutions, have a basis of general knowledge to draw from, use symbols to represent problem concepts, and can work efficiently in a narrow area on hard, challenging problems. An expert system should have some knowledge about how its own system works, and can explain how it arrived at a certain conclusion, including the inferences made and the rationale behind each inference. Finally, as with any human expert, expert systems can make mistakes; however, they can be made to learn from these errors and produce more accurate results the next time.

Expert systems have been used for close to a dozen major tasks. These tasks are described here with examples of what have been done in the past:

Interpretation involves using various sensors to obtain data about a situation, and to make some sense out of this data obtained. Interpreting gauges and readings is one useful application, so is evaluating rock formations and chemical compounds. Even speech and vision systems require interpretation to make out auditory and visual cues for identification.

Prediction is when you have a given situation and you want to determine what might be the likely consequences and results of it. Problems such as a drought, oil shortage, economic changes, military buildup, and insect damage are cases where prediction could be used. These problems involve the techniques of simulation, and are rather difficult to create.

Diagnosis is where you have a problem situation and want to determine the likely causes and characteristics of the problem. The MYCIN expert system previously mentioned is an example of a system that takes on the task of diagnosing problems. Finding problems in all kinds of systems, from electrical circuits to machinery and spacecraft systems, is all part of diagnosis.

Design is an increasingly important area where computers have been employed, and expert systems can be quite useful in designing microprocessors, genes for cloning, organic molecules, and industrial plans.

Planning is closely related to design, and plans are made to find the desired configuration in relation to various constraints. Planning systems also design actions or an entire series of events, such as a military operation.

Monitoring is also important; it can assure if some machine or system is functioning properly. A monitoring system compares an actual system's performance to that of an expected standard. Whether it be a patient in a hospital, the performance of an aircraft, or a nuclear power plant, monitoring is a viable use for expert systems.

Debugging is another application for expert systems, finding faults and problems and suggesting solutions. Debugging is useful for telecommunications systems and electrical equipment. Debugging is useful when there is a simple test for the problem, and when designing remedies and predicting their effectiveness. That is the real power of debugging systems.

Closely related to debugging is the task of **repair**. Repair is exceedingly more complex than debugging systems because actual repair requires a higher degree of knowledge and sophistication and involves diagnosis, debugging, and planning, as well as the control of the appropriate hardware and repair machinery.

Expert systems are also useful for **instruction**. With their knowledge of a field, expert systems diagnose, debug, and repair students' deficiencies. They build a model of what the student understands and analyzes it for deficiencies, then they make plans for correcting these problems, through interaction with the student.

Finally, **control** is a task that combines several of the applications previously mentioned. Depending on the system being controlled, from one to all of the previous functions might need to be implemented in a control system.

Of course, there are various other tasks that can be performed, and instead of elaborating on these, it would be more useful to look at what jobs expert systems have been put to in the real world. The following are summaries of expert systems in various areas and what each of them are designed to do. Keep in mind that all these listings are incomplete, and besides the many others not listed here, new expert systems are being developed all the time.

Medical Expert Systems

Interpretation

PUFF diagnoses the presence of lung disease from pulmonary function test data, including lung capacity and volume, and patient history. Based on lung performance from different disorders, the systems can make determinations as to the patient's probable condition. PUFF was developed at Stanford.

SPE diagnoses inflammatory conditions by interpreting scanning densitomer data. It is designed to detect inflammatory conditions, such as cirrhosis of the liver, through the use of both instrument readings and patient history. This is a forward-chained, rule-based system, developed at Rutgers University. It is now a commercial system.

VM interprets intensive care unit (ICU) patients by interpreting data from equipment. The system detects problems through measurements of heart rate, blood pressure, and readings from a mechanical ventilator. VM, with patient history, can detect possible danger conditions, monitor the patient's state, and suggest strategies. Rule-based, and written in INTERLISP, it was developed at Stanford.

Diagnosis

ABEL diagnoses disorders relating to acid-base and electrolytes. ABEL uses information from both patient history and condition and relationships between different disease states. Knowledge is represented using a type of semantic net. The system was developed at MIT.

AI/COAG diagnoses diseases relating to homeostasis, through the analysis of blood coagulation laboratory tests. It also can evaluate a patient's blood history to confirm the test's diagnosis. AI/COAG was developed at the University of Missouri School of Medicine.

AI/RHEUM diagnoses problems relating to connective tissues and clinical rheumatology. Patient symptoms and lab findings are used to diagnose diseases such as rheumatoid arthritis, sclerosis, and Sjoegren's disease. This is a rule-based system implemented in EXPERT and is a forward-chaining system. It was developed at University of Missouri School of Medicine.

CADACEOUS diagnoses diseases relating to general, internal medicine.

Monitoring

ANNA assists doctors in administering digitalis to those with heart problems. The proper dose is selected and the rate in which it should be given is determined by using patient symptoms and history. After administering the dose, the patient's response is monitored and adjustments are made if necessary. ANNA is written in LISP and was designed at MIT.

Debugging and Diagnosis

BLUE BOX diagnoses and treats clinical depression. Using knowledge from patient's symptoms and drug and medical histories, a management plan is suggested for controlling the depression. This is a rule-based system implemented in EMYCIN and developed at Stanford University.

CASNET/GLAUCOMA diagnoses and offers advice for treating glaucoma and related eye diseases. Using information from test results, symptoms, and other conditions, it provides a narrative interpretation of the case and retrieves references to literature to support its findings. It was developed at Rutgers and is written in FORTRAN.

MYCIN diagnoses and treats bacterial infections. This is a well-known system, and helps physicians select the appropriate antimicrobial therapy for patients with infections of various kinds. The system outputs appropriate drug treatments for these conditions. MYCIN is written in LISP and was developed at Stanford.

ONCOCIN treats and manages cancer patients under chemotherapy. ONCOCIN uses the concept of protocols, selecting therapy suggestions by relating information about a patient's diagnosis, treatment, and lab tests to protocols or experiments that were designed to test the benefits and side effects of various treatments. It is written in INTERLISP and was developed at Stanford.

Instruction

ATTENDING teaches methods of anesthetic practice and management. The system presents the student with a test situation, the student responds, and the student's management plan is critiqued by the system.

GUIDON teaches students how to diagnose and treat patients with bacterial infections. The system selects a case, presents it to the students, and analyzes the students' responses and queries. Then, it matches the students' responses with it own selections.

Geology Expert Systems

LITHO helps geologists to interpret data from oil well logs. It includes a pattern recognition program to obtain features directly from the log. It was developed using EMYCIN.

DRILLING ADVISOR helps oil-rig supervisors to solve the problem of the drill equipment sticking in the borehole during operation. It analyzes the likely causes and recommends treatments.

PROSPECTOR is the well-known system that helps exploration geologists search for ore deposits. It offers the likelihood that particular ore will be found at a location, based upon data about the region. It uses both rules and semantic nets, was developed at SRI International, and was written in INTERLISP.

Chemistry Expert Systems

CRYSALIS uses an electron density map (EDM) to find the three-dimensional structure of a protein. It uses a blackboard architecture, is written in LISP, and was developed at Stanford.

DENDRAL uses mass spectral and nuclear magnetic response data to find the molecular structure of unknown compounds. Developed at Stanford, it is written in INTERLISP.

MOLGEN helps a geneticist plan gene-cloning experiments, creating both an abstract plan and specific steps for implementation in a laboratory. This is both a frame-oriented and object-oriented system, and was written in LISP and UNITS. MOLGEN was developed at Stanford.

SECS helps chemists to synthesize organic molecules. The chemist inputs the desired target molecule, and the system creates a plan for generating it from various "building block" molecules. It is written in FORTRAN and was developed at UC/Santa Cruz.

Computer Expert Systems

DART helps to diagnose faults in computer hardware systems using information about the design being diagnosed. The system takes into account the intended structure and behavior of the device to find design flaws in new devices being created. DART was developed at Stanford, and written using MRS.

XCON is one of the most "mature" of expert systems, and one that has definitely reached commercial status. It decides what must be added to the Vax 11/780 system to create a complete, usable system and considers spatial relationships between all the components. Diagrams that help technicians to assemble the system are created. XCON is rule based, forward chaining, and written in OPS5. It was developed by Carnegie-Mellon and DEC Corporation.

Electronics Expert Systems

ACE locates trouble spots in telephone networks and recommends repair and maintenance. It analyzes maintenance reports, and a host of other factors, before making decisions. A commercial system, it is written in OPS4 and was developed by Bell Laboratories.

PALLADIO helps circuit designers to design and test new VLSI circuits. It has graphics editors, a rule editor, and a simulator that has been used to design different nMOS circuits. Written in LOOPS, it uses object, rule, and logic-oriented knowledge representation. It was developed at Stanford.

SOPHIE teaches students how to troubleshoot electronic circuits. The system demonstrates how to locate a trouble circuit, asks students to predict behavior and perform troubleshooting, and corrects errors with explanations. Developed at Bolt, Berandek, and Newman, it is written in INTERLISP and FORTRAN.

Engineering Expert Systems

REACTOR helps engineers diagnose and treat nuclear reactor accidents. It monitors instruments such as feed-water flow, radiation level, and evaluates the situation if a problem occurs. Written in LISP, it is a rule-based system with forward and backward chaining.

DELTA is used to find and correct problems with diesel locomotives using diagnostic strategies. The system helps technicians through the repair process, with diagrams, instructions, and even videodisk movies. Written in LISP (and later FORTH), it was developed by General Electric.

Military Expert Systems

ADEPT is designed to perform situation assessment reports by interpreting intelligence sensor reports.

HANNIBAL is designed for situation assessment in terms of communications intelligence, identifying enemy organizational units, and interpreting data from sensors.

Other expert systems include the following, which are described in various books on the subject:

- ☐ Agriculture: PLANT/CD, PLANT/DS, POMME
- ☐ Law: AUDITOR, DSCAS, JUDITH, LEGAL ANALYSIS SYSTEM, LRS
- ☐ Manufacturing: IMACS, ISIS, PTRANS
- ☐ Mathematics: ADVISOR, MATHLAB68

- Meteorology: WILLARD
- Physics: GAMMA, MECHO
- Process Control: FALCON, PDS
- Space Technology: FAITH, LES, NAVEX, RBMS, RPMS

Many others exist, so consult a reference book on this subject for additional information on all the expert systems available.

Knowledge Representation

Now that you have a good idea of what expert systems are, and what kinds of work they can do, it's time to look a bit further at how knowledge is represented inside the system. There are three main methods of representing knowledge: rules, frames, and semantic nets.

Rules are a method whereby strategies, instructions, and recommendations can be represented in a direct, formal way. Rules in expert systems are even more formal than that used by people, and as conditional statements in conventional programming languages, follow an IF...THEN format. The knowledge contained in these rules is checked against the information gathered about a particular situation. If a match exists, and the IF portion is satisfied, then the second part, the THEN segment, is performed. The rule is then said to execute or fire.

Naturally, for an expert system to be of any significant use, many rules must be checked against the information at hand. One action taken when a rule fires is to modify the set of facts in the knowledge base. When several IF statements are matched to the facts and successive execution (firing) of rules occurs, we have what is known as an inference chain. This brings together several related matched facts, which are successively linked together by adding additional rules, to form an entire sequence that can bring forth a certain conclusion or action. See FIG. 11-2 for a diagram of a rule-based inference chain.

There are two main methods of chaining—forward chaining and backward chaining. As you might guess, they work in different ways, and are applicable in different situations. Forward chaining is when you have a group of facts, and you match these facts to the rules in your knowledge base to form new facts. In a sense, you are using the facts available to obtain new information that is added to the knowledge base, and after several matches, you find that a given situation, let's call it A, does exist.

168 Expert Systems

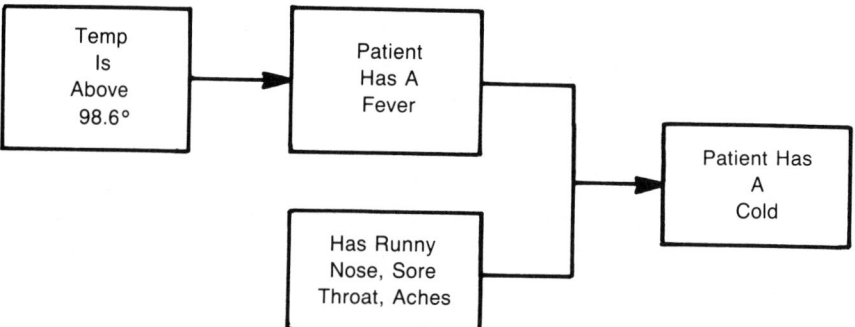

Fig. 11-2. Inference chain. A simple representation of an inference chain.

Backward chaining proceeds in a different way. In this case you start with what you want to prove, such as situation A, and only execute rules that are relevant to proving A. In the end, the two approaches give similar results, however, the methods of solving the problem are different.

Semantic nets are an entirely different method of representing knowledge. The main concept behind these is the network structure, which was originally used to represent human memory. In simplest terms, a semantic net consists of nodes linked together by arcs that describe the relationships between the nodes. Each node can represent a thing, event, concept, person, or something related. The arcs that show the relationships between these nodes usually have such properties as *isa* and *has part*. This is very easy to understand, such as in the examples "747 isa plane" and "plane *has-part* engine." This type of network structure also has "inheritance properties" where nodes lower in the net take on properties of those higher up. In other words, the upper nodes represent the more general concepts while the lower nodes represent more specific cases and instances of these general concepts.

The benefit of the semantic net is that it can be searched to find various nodes deep within the structure and also determine quickly the relationship between them. This is especially useful for natural language applications, because the complex grammar and structure of English can be represented using this network and used to interpret it successfully. See FIG. 11-3 for a diagram of a semantic net, and FIG. 11-4 for a natural language semantic net.

Frames are another major method of representing knowledge. A frame could be described as a specific type of data structure where attached to each frame several kinds and pieces of information are stored.

Knowledge Representation   169

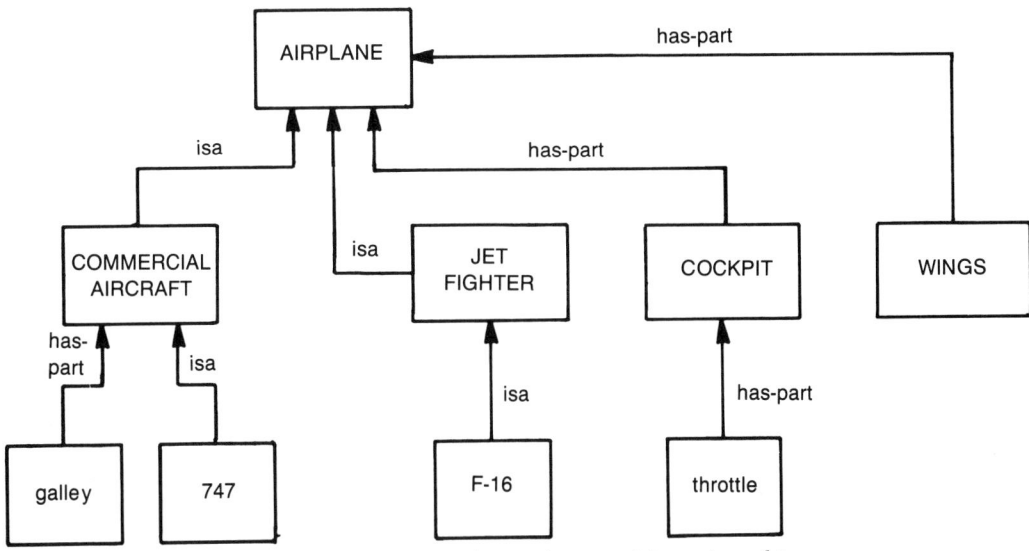

Fig. 11-3. Semantic net. This is a semantic net for airplanes and its parts and types.

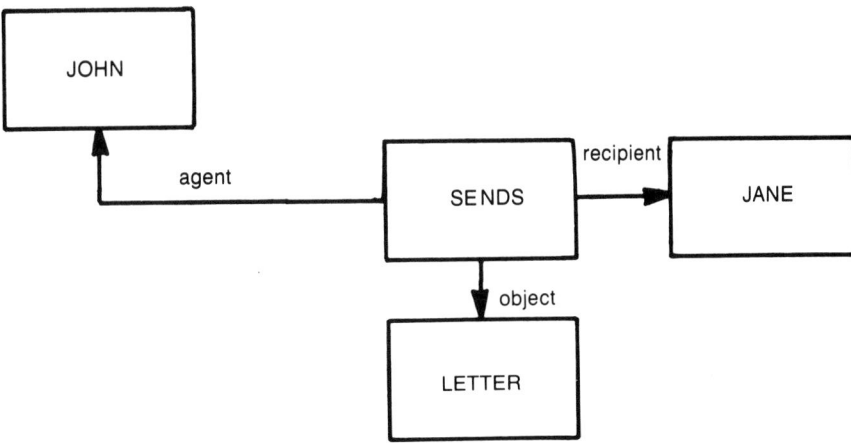

Fig. 11-4. Semantic net—natural language. A semantic net for a natural language situation involving sending a letter.

The organization of a semantic net is similar to that of a natural language, semantic net with nodes connected by relations, and the more general frames at the top.

Each node in a frame-based system is defined by a collection of attributes and the value (specific instances) of each, which are known in general as "slots." This could be visualized as a form of "mailbox" where there are slots for various pieces of information. Attributes could be name, age, and occupation, while the values of them could be John, 35, and dentist. In addition, a slot can have procedures that contain computer code, which are executed whenever information in that slot is changed. There might be some task to be completed when information is added, when it is deleted, and when information is needed, but it is empty. See FIG. 11-5 for a diagram of a frame.

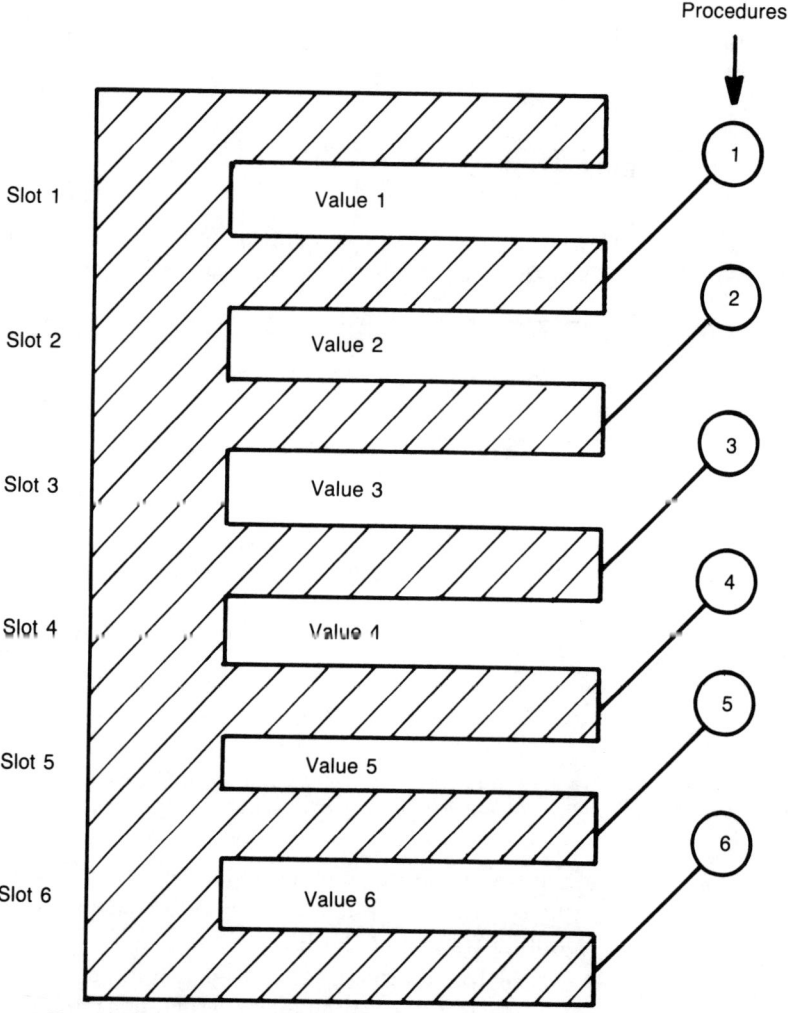

Fig. 11-5. Frame. The representation of a frame for knowledge representation. Values are places in one or more of the six slots.

Rules, frames, and semantic nets are the major ways in which information is represented in expert systems. Each has its own strengths and weaknesses, and appropriateness for certain types of expert systems.

As you probably understand by now, creating an expert system is far more complex than writing a COBOL application program. It requires not only the representation of knowledge (the knowledge base), but expertise in making that information accessible to the user of the system through various problem-solving techniques (inference engine). Creating an expert system requires not only the use of various experts and professionals, but also special programs and languages known as expert systems tools. The next section will describe these tools and how they help to create expert systems.

Expert Systems Tools

Expert systems tools help knowledge engineers to handle the difficult task of creating an expert system. There is not just one type of tool, but an entire range of products ranging from high-level programming languages to low-level support facilities. There are four major types of expert systems tools: programming languages, languages for knowledge engineering, system creation aids, and support facilities. Each of these categories will be discussed in detail.

Programming languages are either procedure oriented or symbol oriented. Procedure-oriented languages are the conventional programming languages such as FORTRAN or Pascal, and deal with specific types of problems, for example FORTRAN is especially suited to mathematical problems. On the other hand, symbol-manipulation languages are designed for artificial intelligence applications. LISP and PROLOG fall into this category. For more information on programming languages, consult the chapter on languages in this book.

Languages for knowledge engineering differ from programming languages in that they are specifically designed for developing expert systems. These languages usually include an expert systems building language together with an integrated support environment. There are two types of knowledge engineering languages, skeletal and general purpose. A skeletal language is a stripped-down expert system, which has its inference engine, but without its knowledge base. For instance, in order to create KAS, a skeletal system for classification and diagnosis, the creators took out the knowledge about geology found in PROSPEC-

TOR. Similarly, they used MYCIN to create the skeletal system EMYCIN, known as "Empty Mycin." The benefits of skeletal systems include an established structure, applicable facilities, and an inference engine that is proven useful for a certain type of operation. However, they are not very flexible and general, and are restricted to a certain class of problems.

On the other hand, a general purpose knowledge engineering language can handle many more different types of problems. You can have more control over searching and data access; however, the language might be more difficult to use. There are both research and commercial versions available.

System Building Aids, as the name suggests, help build expert systems. There are systems building aids that address the problem of acquiring and representing knowledge, and others that assist in the design of expert systems themselves. Compared to tools in the other categories, relatively few have been built in this category. TEIRESIAS (knowledge acquisition) helps bridge the transfer of knowledge from a human domain expert to a computer knowledge base through the use of English-like statements. The rules are analyzed, suggestions are made concerning them, and TEIRESIAS assists in adding the rule to the knowledge base. AGE, on the other hand, is a tool for system design, and consists of a set of components that can be put together to form parts of an expert system. Components (written in INTERLISP) support certain tasks and functions, such as forward chaining, blackboard architecture, or backward chaining. AGE was used to build the expert system known as HANNIBAL, which interpreted enemy radio communications for situation assessment. This is primarily a research system for a knowledge engineer with a knowledge of INTERLISP programming.

Support facilities include all other tools that knowledge engineers use to create expert systems. This includes debugging aids, input/output facilities, explanation facilities, and knowledge base editors.

Debugging aids are useful to help discover and correct errors within expert systems. Tracing programs can trace a sequence of rules fired to help find errors and follow the execution of the program. A break package can be used to tell the program where to stop, such as right before some error has occurred. These two are very basic and necessary aids. With an automated testing program, you can test a program on a number of benchmark problems to uncover errors and difficulties with the system.

Input/Output, or I/O, facilities help make working the system easier. There is run-time knowledge acquisition where the user can converse real-time with the running expert systems. Menus also can be implemented to make the process of using the system easier. Other routines allow you to access the operating system and other parts of the computer if necessary.

Explanation facilities are also quite useful. An answer or suggestion is not always clear, and you might want to know how the system came to that conclusion. Different systems and tools have different facilities for doing this; however, there are three basic ways that expert systems can explain themselves: retrospective, hypothetical, and counterfactual reasoning.

Retrospective will trace back to rules and inference chains to explain how it came to that conclusion. Hypothetical is the method where the system can explain what would have happened differently if a certain fact or rule had been different. Finally, counterfactual reasoning will show why it came up with a certain conclusion when the expected conclusion was not reached.

Finally, there are expert systems tools that edit the knowledge base (text editors), perform automatic bookkeeping of changes to the system, check syntax to ensure that the right format for rules has been used, and check consistency for determining if the newly entered rules conflict with or contradict with those already in the knowledge base.

These are the major expert systems tools in use and more are being developed every day. In any case, the main goal of these programs is to help do what is the topic of the next section: build an expert system.

Building an Expert System

Building an expert system is a complex and difficult task. Even with the tools previously mentioned, getting knowledge from human experts and putting them into a computer (and creating the inference engine) is no easy task. However, great strides are being made in this field, and many dozens of professional expert systems are in use today.

What are the steps for designing and implementing an expert system? In general, there are five main steps, which are listed below:

Identification In this step, the knowledge engineer and domain expert work on defining the problem. They also decide what experts and persons should be involved, what resources are needed, the goals and objectives, and any other matters that need to be planned and considered.

Conceptualization Now, the task turns to a more specific level, and the objective here is to determine what concepts, ideas, relationships, and strategies should be used to describe data in the system. An issue of importance is granularity, which refers to what level of detail the knowledge should be represented.

Formalization Here, work begins on expressing the key concepts and relationships in a formal way, often by using an expert system building language. The type of approach, whether rule, frame, or other method, is considered. In general, all the tools and techniques needed to produce the expert system is designed and laid out.

Implementation Now, all the plans made are put into action with the actual building of the computer program. The use of all plans preceding this point is important, including the methods for specifying the information, integration of all parts, creating an efficient running expert system. The completion of a prototype is a good way to test the system before making final changes.

Testing The final stage of development includes an evaluation of the performance and usability of the program, searching for places where revisions are necessary, and running the system on a wide variety of problems to determine how well it works in various situations. Questions that can be asked include, are decisions appropriate, are inference rules correct and consistent, is the method of querying the system easy to use, and are the explanations given adequate and correct?

Finally, after testing and evaluating of the prototype, further refinements can be made, after which it can be sent for field testing before being released for commercial use.

In general, there are five main stages an expert system must go through: a demonstration prototype to show the usefulness of the system and also test its efficiency so far (50-100 rules); a research prototype that is designed for more rigorous testing on test cases (200-500 rules); a field prototype that can be tested on real world problems (500-1000 rules); a production prototype; and a commercial system.

Production prototypes have been field tested exhaustively, and frequently are recoded into a different language to improve efficiency. At this point, with 500-1500 rules, it can function very efficiently, and is very close to the point of being ready for commercial use. Finally, commercial systems are production prototypes that have been acquired for use on a commercial basis. XCON, with over 3000 rules, is close to 95 percent accurate, and is the most well-known example of an expert system in commercial use.

The field of expert systems is one of the most significant among all areas of artificial intelligence, and much research has been done in this area. Now that you are familiar with the process of expert systems design, you can find out what research has been done in recent years.

Expert Systems Research

Expert systems research is going on through the country, and overseas. For example, in the United States, there are literally hundreds of places involved in some phase of expert systems, with the major work being done at universities, research centers, and knowledge engineering companies. This section will attempt to look at some of the work that is being done and what has been accomplished so far.

Many universities across the country offer programs in AI, and of these, a number have done concentrated research in the area of expert systems. However, only a handful account for most of the research in this area. Stanford, Carnegie-Mellon, and MIT are indisputably the leaders in the AI research, and the first two have placed much of their efforts on knowledge engineering and expert systems.

In fact, Stanford has been the center of development for such systems and tools as DENDRAL, MYCIN, BLUE BOX, FOLIO, HASP, ONCOCIN, PUFF, ROGET, SACON, UNITS, VM, and TEIRESIAS. Their focus has been in the areas of medicine, chemistry, computer systems, management science, engineering, and electronics. Edward Feigenbaum, a leader in the field, coined the term knowledge engineering, and the work on DENDRAL led to the term knowledge-based system. Carnegie-Mellon worked on the successful system XCON, as well as several others including CALLISO, DAA, MUD, PDS, SRL, and XSEL. Their fields of concentration include computer systems, manufacturing, military applications, process controls, and electronics. Rutgers (medicine, geology, law, electronics), MIT (medicine and mathematics), and the University of Illinois at Urbana, Illinois (agriculture, law, medicine) also are centers of research in this area.

Research organizations also have worked extensively in the development of expert systems, the major players being the Rand Corporation, Xerox, Advanced Information and Decision Systems (AI&DS), and Ford Aerospace.

The Rand Corporation has devoted much of its energies to expert systems tools and applications, especially in the areas of military applications, being funded in part by DARPA. ROSIE, a well-known knowledge engineering language, was developed here, as well as LDS, SCENARIO, AGENT, SWIRL, RITA, and ROSS.

Xerox, at its Palo Alto Research Center, known as PARC, has concentrated on languages and tools, developing INTERLISP, KRL, LOOPS, and SMALLTALK-80. Finally, AI&DS develops expert systems for military use, such as radar signal analysis, faults in aircraft navigation systems, and related tasks.

Finally, knowledge engineering companies also contribute to the furthering of expert systems development. APEX, Applied Expert Systems, serves the financial services industry with its AI-based financial packages. Carnegie Group, of Pittsburgh, develops systems and tools for industry and manufacturing, including SRL+ and PLUME. Intellicorp works on expert systems and tools for the biotechnology and genetic engineering field, while Syntelligence is also in expert systems building for financial applications. Teknowledge is another leader in this field, having developed the M.1 and S.1 knowledge engineering languages. Other firms that have done work in this field include Computer*Thought Corporation, Inference Corp., Production Systems Technologies, and Software A&E.

The field of expert systems is expanding, and as more work is done in this area, you will find computerized experts in more and more fields and industries. This is one of the most promising areas of AI and the fifth generation, and one that will be of considerable benefit to persons of all careers and backgrounds.

Index

A

ABEL expert systems, 163
ACE expert systems, 165
actuators, robotics, 119
ADEPT, 166
advanced architectures, 8, 16-18, 21, 31
Advanced Digital Radar Imagery Exploitation System (ADRIES), USA, 19
Advanced Information and Decision System (AI/DS), 176
advanced information processing, 25, 26, 27
Advanced Micro Devices Corp., 22
ADVISOR expert systems, 166
AEG, 25
AGE toolkit, 172
AGENT, 176
agricultural expert systems, 166
AI/COAG expert systems, 163
AI/RHEUM expert systems, 163
Air-Land Battle Management System (ALBM), USA, 13, 16
Aiso, Hideo, 6
Aix-Marseille University, 136
Alvey of Great Britain, 7, 27-30
Alvey, John, 7, 27
ambiguity, natural languages and, 148
AMORD, 141
Anadigics, 66
Angel speech recognition system, 19
ANNA expert systems, 163
applications (see software and)
Applied Expert Systems, 176
architectures
    advanced, 8, 21, 31
    binary tree, 47, 48
    bus-based, 47, 48-49
    dataflow, 52
    multiprocessor, 18
    n-dimensional cube, 49-51
    parallel processing, 41-45
    pipelining, 43-44
    USA research in, 16-18
    vector processing, 44-45
arithmetic primitives, LISP, 128
Arizona University, 68
Army Advanced Ground Vehicle Technology program, USA, 15
articulated coordinate programming languages arm, 116
artificial intelligence, 8, 21, 27, 52, 91, 95, 102, 124
    artificial vision and, 106
    LISP and, 133
    natural languages and, 150
    robotics and, 120
Asimov, Isaac, 109
AT&T (see Bell Labs)
atoms, LISP, 125
ATTENDING expert systems, 164
AUDITOR expert systems, 166
Augmented Transition Network, 147
automatic dictation, speech recognition and, 81
Autonomous Land Vehicle, USA, 13, 15-16
avionics, Pilot's Associate and, 14

B

ballistic transistor, 58, 62
BASIC, 124, 125
Belgian Institute of Management, 26
Bell Labs, 62, 66, 68, 71, 72, 73, 166
Bellman, Richard, 85
Berkeley University, 18
binary tree architecture, 47, 48

blackboard, speech recognition and, 87
"block world," vision systems and, 102
BLUE BOX expert systems, 163, 175
Boardman, Derek, 30
Boeing Electronics, 22, 68
Bolt, Bernadek and Newman, 17, 86, 87, 125, 147, 166
bottlenecks
　bus-based architectures, 48
　von Neumann, 43
Bresnan, Joan, 150
British Telecom, 7, 27, 88
Bull, 25, 26
Burroughs Corporation, 65
bus-based architecture, 48-49
　distributed memory and, 49
　global memory and, 48
　shared memory and, 49
Butterfly, 17

C

CAD/CAM, 30
CADACEOUS expert systems, 163
CALLISO expert systems, 175
CalTech, 105
Cambridge University, 28, 73, 88
Carnegie Group, 176
Carnegie-Mellon University, 16, 17, 18, 19, 87, 175
cartesian coordinate robotics arm, 114
CASNET/GLAUCOMA expert systems, 164
chaining, 167
chemical expert systems, 165
CMOS technology, 26, 28
Colmeraur, 7
Combat Action Team (CAT), ALBM and, 16
Common LISP, 125
Compact LISP Machine, 18
compilers, 29
computer aided design (CAD), 12, 21, 22, 26, 30
computer expert systems, 165
computer integrated manufacturing, 26, 27
Computer Thought Corp., 176
computer vision technology, 95-104
　"block world" and, 102
　controlled hallucination and, 104
　edge detection for, 98

heterarchial constraint propagation, 103
knowledge representation and, 102
knowledge-directed vision, 96
Marr theories for, 96-99
primal sketch and, 97
segmentation and, 97
signal processing for, 98
computer-integrated manufacturing, 25
conjunctions, PROLOG, 139
Connection Machine, 17
　hypercube architecture and, 50
CONNIVER, 141
CONS cells, LISP and, 126
context-free parsing, 147
Control Data Corporation, 7, 20, 43, 45
controlled hallucination, vision systems and, 104
controllers, robotics, 119
Cornell University, 62
Cray supercomputers, 26
Cray X-MP48, 48
Cray X/MP, 17
Cray-1, 41, 45, 48
Cray-2, 39, 41
Cray-MXP, 41
CRYSALIS expert systems, 165
Currey University, 28
cyborgs, 111
cylindrical coordinate robotics arm, 114

D

DAA expert systems, 175
DART expert systems, 165
data entry, speech recognition and, 81
database management, 12, 21, 52
dataflow architecture, 52
decision making, programming languages and, 133
Dedale, 30
deep structure, natural languages and, 149
Defense Advanced Research Projects Agency (DARPA), 7, 15, 176
　image analysis and, 19
　speech recognition and, 86
　Strategic Computing Initiative, 12
DELTA relational database manage-

ment machine, 9, 166
DENDRAL expert systems, 165, 175
Dennis, Jack, 52
Dertouzos, Michael L., 7, 42
direct template matching, speech recognition and, 85
distributed memory, 49
documentation, expert systems for, 158
domain knowledge, expert systems and, 159
doping, 59
Dove, Grant A., 21
DRILLING ADVISOR expert systems, 164
DSCAS expert systems, 166
DuPont, 68

E

edge detection, 98-99
Edinburgh University, 28, 29
electron-beam technology, photolithography and, 64
Electronic Dictionary, 9
electronic mail, EuroCom, 26
electronics expert systems, 165-166
Electronique Serge Dassault (ESD), France, 30
EMV Associates, 75
EMYCIN expert systems, 164, 172
end effectors, robotics, 117
engineering expert systems, 166
ENIAC, 42
environments, 28
Equips, 28
EuroCom electronic mail and conferencing, 26
European Computer Research Center (ECRC), 26
European fifth-generation technology research, 23-35
    Alvey of Great Britain, 27-30
    ESPRIT, 24-27
    European Strategic Plan for Research, 8
    Japan, 7
    SICO of France, 30-31
    USSR and Eastern Europe, 31-34
    West Germany in, 31
    Western Europe in, 24
European Strategic Plan for Research in Infor Tech (ESPRIT), 8, 24-27

expert systems, 26, 27, 30, 155-176
    Advanced Information and Decision System (AI/DS), 176
    agricultural, 166
    Alvey of Great Britain and, 28
    applications for, 160-162
    Autonomous Land Vehicle, 16
    building of, 173-175
    chaining, 167
    chemical, 165
    computer, 165
    Dedale and, 30
    electronics, 165-166
    engineering, 166
    explanation facilities for, 173
    frames in, 135, 168
    geological, 164-165
    I/O facilities for, 173
    inference engines and, 159
    knowledge base of, 159
    knowledge representation in, 167
    law, 166
    manufacturing, 166
    mathematics, 166
    medical applications, 162-164
    meteorology, 167
    military, 166-167
    physics, 167
    problems facing, 158
    process control, 167
    programming languages for, 171
    Proteus shell, 21
    research in, 175-176
    retrospective facilities for, 173
    rules in, 134, 167
    selection of, 157-159
    semantic nets, 168
    space technology, 167
    structure of, 159
    system building aids, 172
    TEIRESIAS, 172
    text editors, 173
    toolkits for, 29, 171
Expert Systems Community Clubs, Great Britain, 28

F

Fabry, Charles, 70
Fabry-Perot interferometer, 70
FAITH expert systems, 167
FALCON expert systems, 167
feature detector, vision systems and, 105
Feigenbaum, Edward, 7, 175

Ferranti, 30
Fifth Generation Computer Project, 4-6
  international cooperation in, 7
  Lexical Functional Grammar (LFG) and, 150
  research areas in, 8
Fillmore, Charles, 149
filtering, speech recognition and, 84
Flagship Project, Great Britain, 29
FLAVORS, 141
FOLIO expert systems, 175
Force Requirements Expert System (FRESH), ALBM and, 16
Ford, 66
Forest, 28
FORTH, 166
FORTRAN, 125, 164, 165, 166, 171
frames
  expert systems and, 168
  LISP, 135
FRL, 141, 142
Fuchi, Kazuhiro, 6
Fujitsu, 5, 66, 68

G

gallium arsenide, 66-67
GAMMA expert systems, 167
Gaussian filters, vision systems and, 99
GEC, 28
General Electric, 166
General Motors, 95
geological expert systems, 164-165
GigaBit Logic, 66
global memory, bus-based architecture and, 48
granularity, 46
graph reduction in parallel (GRIP), 29
GTE, 68
GUIDON expert systems, 164

H

handicapped machines, speech recognition and, 91
HANNIBAL expert systems, 166, 172
hardware and technologies, 37-120
  microchips, 57-78, 57
  parallel processing, 39-56
  robotics, 109-120
  speech recognition, 79-90
  vision systems, 91-107
HARPY speech recognition system, 87
Harris Corporation, 22
HASP expert systems, 175
Hear What I Mean (HWIM) speech recognition system, 87
HEARSAY speech recognition system, 87
high-electron-mobility transistor (HEMT), 39, 58, 60-62
  electron movement within, 61
Heriot-Watt University, 68, 69, 71
heterarchial constraint propagation, vision systems and, 103
heterostructures, 61
Hitachi, 5, 68
Honeywell, 19
Honeywell Bull company, 21
Huang, Alan, 71
Hubel, David, 105
Hughes, 78
human factors technology, 12, 21, 29
hypercube (see n-dimensional cube architecture)
hypertext systems, Plane-Text/FIG system, 22
Hypertron supercomputer, USSR, 33

I

IBM, 43, 62, 65, 66, 68, 73, 76, 88, 105
ICL, 25, 26, 29, 30
ICOT, 9
Illinois University, 62, 175
image processing (see also vision systems), 26, 59
  parallel processing and, 45
  USA research in, 19-20
Imperial College, 29
Inference Corp., 176
inference engine, 159
  knowledge-based machine and, 9
information processing, 31
  advanced, 25, 26, 27
Inman, Bobby, 21
Institute of New Generation Computer Technology (ICOT), Japan, 6
integrated circuits, 31
  CMOS, 26, 28

micrometer bipolar, 26, 28
Intellicorp, 176
INTERLISP, 125, 163, 164, 165, 166, 172, 176
International Committee for Computer Engineering (ICCE), USSR, 32
island driving, speech recognition and, 86
iWARP system, 17, 18

J

Japan Information Processing Development Assoc. (JIPDEC), 5
Japanese fifth-generation technology research, 3-9
  Fifth Generation Computer Project, 4, 5, 6, 8
  Institute of New Generation Computers, 6
  international response to, 7
  Japan's Information Processing Development project, 5
  Next-Generation Industries Project, 4, 5
  research areas in, 8
  Superspeed Computer Project, 4, 5
Jelinek, Frederick, 88
Johns Hopkins University, 77
Joint Speech Research Unit, Great Britain, 88
jointed coordinate robotics arm, 116
Josephson junctions, 39, 59, 72-75, 78
Josephson, Brian, 73
JUDITH expert systems, 166

K

Kapek, Karel, 109
Kaplan, Ronald, 150
Karatsu, Hajime, 6
KAS programming language, 171
knowledge base, expert systems and, 159
knowledge engineering, 26, 157, 176
knowledge representation
  expert systems and, 167
  vision systems and, 102
knowledge-based machine, 9
knowledge-based systems, 12, 21, 27, 31
knowledge-directed vision, 96
KRL, 141, 142, 176
Kurzweil Computer Products, 89
Kurzweil, Raymond, 89

L

language development, 26
  parallel processing and, 54
laser technology (see optical interconnections, photochromic molecules
law expert systems, 166
LDS, 176
LEGAL ANALYSIS SYSTEM expert systems, 166
LES expert systems, 167
lexical analysis, natural languages and, 146
Lexical Functional Grammar (LFG), natural languages and, 150
linear predictive analysis, speech recognition and, 84
Linsker, Ralph, 105
LISP, 26, 29, 124-125, 142, 165
  AI applications, 133
  arithmetic primitives, 128
  assigning values: SETQ in, 132
  building blocks of, atoms and lists, 125-126
  CONS cells in, 126
  creating your own functions in, 132
  decision making, 133
  frames, 135
  list representation in, 126-127, 130-132, 134
  predicates in, 129
  procedures and functions in, 127
  rules and, 134
LISP machines, 18
LISP workstation, 9
lists, LISP, 126, 134
LITHO expert systems, 164
Lockheed-Georgia, 13
Logica, 29, 88
Logos speech analyzer, 88, 140
LOKI, 26
Loops speech recognition system, 88, 141, 142, 176
LRS expert systems, 166
Lytel, 66

M

M.1 knowledge engineering language, 176
Mach operating system, 18
machine intelligence, 12
machine operations, speech recognition and, 81
machine vision (see also vision systems), 104-107
    AI and, 106
    feature detector and, 105
    RET-30, 105
MACLISP, 125
MAMO, East Germany, 34
man-machine interfaces, 7, 27
    Autonomous Land Vehicle and, 15
    Pilot's Associate and, 15
Manchester University, 28, 29
manipulator arms, robotics, 114-117
manufacturing expert systems, 166
Mariane Project, 30
Marr, David, 96, 97, 103
Martin Marietta, 15
Maryland University, 75
mathematical expert systems, 166
MATHLAB68 expert systems, 166
Matsushita Tsushin Company, 6, 68
McCarthy, John, 124
McDonnell Douglas, 13
Mead, Carver, 105
MECHO expert systems, 167
medical expert systems, 162-164
memory
    distributed, 49
    global, bus-based architecture and, 48
    shared, 49
mesh schemes, parallel processing and, 46, 47
meteorology expert systems, 167
microchip technology, 57-78
    ballistic transistor, 58, 62
    gallium arsenide, 66-67
    HEMT, 58, 60-62
    Josephson junctions, 72-75
    molecular technologies, 75-78
    optical technologies, 68-72
    photochromic molecules, 77-78
    photolithography, 63-64
    SEED, 71-72
    semiconductor technologies, 59-67
    superconductivity and, 59
    transphasor, 69-71
    wafer-scale integration, 64-66
Microcomputer and Computer technology (MCC), USA, 7, 12, 20-22
microelectronics, 12, 21, 25
micrometer bipolar ICs, 26, 28
military expert systems, 166-167
Miller, David, 72
MIPS Computer Systems, 18
mission and flight planning, Pilot's Associate, 14
Mississippi University, 75
Missouri University, 163
MIT Laboratories, 42, 52, 89, 96, 104, 125, 163, 175
Mitsubishi, 5, 9
molecular rectifier, 75-77
molecular technologies, 75-78
    molecular rectifier, 75-77
    photochromic molecules, 77-78
MOLGEN expert systems, 165
morphological analysis, natural languages and, 146
Mosaic Systems, 65
Moto-oka, Tohru, 6
Motorola, 66
MUD expert systems, 175
multiple-instruction-stream/multiple-data-stream, 49
multiprocessor architectures, 18
MYCIN expert systems, 164, 172, 175

N

n-dimensional cube architecture, 49-51
National Bureau of Standards, 73
National Information Processing Laboratory (INRIA), France, 7
National Science Foundation, 75
natural languages, 12, 15, 16, 18, 27, 143-153
    ambiguity in, 148
    Augmented Transition Network, 147
    deep structure, 149
    Lexical Functional Grammar (LFG), 150
    machine translation of, 145
    parsing and, 147
    Plan Applier Mechanism (PAM), 153

pragmatics and, 152
Script Applier Machine (SAM), 153
scripts in, 152
semantics and, 150
syntax in, 146
Naval Ocean Systems Center, 16
Naval Research Laboratory, 75
NAVEX expert systems, 167
NCR Design Advisor, 22
NCUBE/seven parallel processing system, 53
NEC, 5, 21, 66, 68
Next-Generation Industries Project, Japan's, 4, 5
Nixdorf, 25
Norris, William, 20

O

office automation, 25, 26, 27
Oki, 5, 9
Olivetti, 25
ONCOCIN expert systems, 164, 175
Open University, 29
open-loop robotics controllers, 119
OPS5, 141
Optical Circuit Cooperative, 68
optical interconnections, 19
optical technologies (see also vision systems), 68-72
    SEED, 71-72
    transphasor, 69-71
optical transistor, 69
Orchidee battlefield surveillance systems, France, 31
Oxford University, 28

P

PALLADIO expert systems, 166
Palo Alto Research Center (PARC), 150, 176
parallel processing, 12, 16, 17, 21, 29, 31, 39-56
    architectures for, 41-45
    benchmarks for, 56
    binary tree architecture, 47, 48
    bus-based architecture, 47, 48-49
    Cray supercomputers and, 41
    dataflow architecture and, 52
    ENIAC and, 42
    future of, 45-47
    granularity and, 46
    hard- and software errors in, 55
    image processing and, 45
    mesh schemes for, 46, 47
    n-dimensional cube architecture, 49-51
    NCUBE/seven, 53
    pipelining, 43-44
    programming for, 54-56
    ring networks for, 46, 47
    standardization, lack of, 56
    vector processing, 44-45
    VLSI and, 39
    von Neumann machines and, 42
parsing, natural languages and, 147
Pascal, 124, 171
pattern matching and searching
    programming languages and, 136
    vision systems and, 95, 96
PDS expert systems, 167, 175
Pennsylvania University, 42
Perot, Albert, 70
Phillips, 25
phonemes, 86
phonemic unit, 86
photochromic molecules, 77-78
photolithography, 63-64
physics expert systems, 167
Pilot's Associate, USA, 13-15
pipelining, parallel processing and, 43-44
Pivot III-V, 66
Plan Applier Mechanism (PAM), 153
Plane-Text/FIG hypertext system, 22
PLANNER, 141
PLANT/CD expert systems, 166
PLANT/DS expert systems, 166
Plessey, 25, 28, 30
PLUME, 176
polar coordinate robotics arm, 115
POMME expert systems, 166
POP-2, 141
POPLER, 141
Portable Computer Tool Environment (PCTE) interface, 26
Portable Standard LISP, 125
pragmatics, natural languages and, 152
Praxis, 30
predicates, LISP, 129
primal sketch, vision systems and, 97
process control expert systems, 167
Production Systems Technologies, 176

programming, parallel processing, 54-56
programming languages, 123-142
  AMORD, 141
  CONNIVER, 141
  decision making, 133
  expert systems and, 171, 176
  FLAVORS, 141
  FRL, 141
  KAS, 171
  KRL, 141
  LISP, 124-125
  LOGO, 140
  LOOPS, 141
  OPS5, 141
  pattern matching and searching, 136
  PLANNER, 141
  POP-2, 141
  POPLER, 141
  PROLOG, 136
  Simula, 141
  Smalltalk, 141
  Stanford Artificial Intelligence Language (SAIL), 141
PROLOG, 9, 26, 29, 136
  asking questions with, 138
  conjuctions with, 139
  mathematical operations in, 140
property lists, 134
PROSPECTOR expert systems, 164, 171
Proteus expert-system shell, 21
PSI logic-programming machine, 9
PUFF expert systems, 162, 175

Q
question asking, PROLOG, 138

R
Racal, 30
Rand Corporation, 175, 176
RBMS expert systems, 167
RCA, 66
REACTOR expert systems, 166
rectangular coordinate robotics arm, 114
rectifier, molecular, 75-77
Reduced-Instruction Set Computers (RISC), 18
relational database management machine (DELTA), 9
remote access systems, speech recognition and, 81

research, 1-36
  Europe and, 23-36
  Japan and, 3-9
  United states and, 11-22
  USSR and Eastern Europe, 31-34
RET-30 artificial retina, 105
Rich, Elaine, 150
ring networks, parallel processing and, 46, 47
risk analysis, 28
RITA, 176
robotics, 26, 34, 109-120
  actuators, 114
  controllers, 119
  end effectors, 117
  fictional use of, 109
  industrial applications, 111-114
  manipulator arms, 114-117
  operation of, 114-119
  senses and intelligence, 120
Robotron typewriters, East Germany, 34
Rockefeller Foundation, 144
Rockwell International, 66
ROGET expert systems, 175
ROSIE, 176
ROSS, 176
Royal Signals and Radar Establishment, 30
RPMS expert systems, 167
rules
  expert systems, 167
  LISP, 134
Rutgers University, 163

S
6600 microprocessor, 43
7600 microprocessor, 45
S.1 knowledge engineering language, 176
SACON expert systems, 175
Schank, Roger, 150, 152, 153
Script Applier Machine (SAM), 150
scripts, natural languages and, 152
SCS, 27
searching, programming languages and, 136
SECS expert systems, 165
segmentation
  speech recognition and, 85, 86
  vision systems and, 97
selective compliance robot assembly arm (SCARA), 117, 118
self-electro-optic effect device (SEED), 58, 71-72, 78

semantic nets, expert systems and, 168
semantic primitives, 150
semantics, natural languages and, 150
Semiconductor Research Corporation (SRC), USA, 12
semiconductor technologies, 59-67
  ballistic transistors, 62
  gallium arsenide, 66-67
  HEMT, 60-62
  photolithography, 63-64
  wafer-scale integration, 64-66
sensors research, 19
servomechanism robotics controllers, 119
shared memory, 49
Shelley, Mary, 109
SICO of France, 7, 30-31
Siconflex, 27
Siemens, 25, 26, 27
silicon, 59
  gallium arsenide vs., 66
Simula, 141
single-instruction/multiple-data (SIMD) processing, 49
skeletal language, 171
Smalltalk, 141, 176
Software A/E, 176
software and applications, 8, 21, 25, 27, 29, 30, 121-177
  expert systems, 155-176
  natural languages, 143-154
  programming languages, 123-142
solitons, 76, 77, 78
SOPHIE expert systems, 166
Southampton University, 28
Southern California, University of, 85
Soviet Union (see USSR and Eastern Europe)
space technology expert systems, 167
SPE expert systems, 162
speech recognition, 12, 15, 16, 26, 28, 30, 59, 79-90
  advantages of, 80
  applications for, 81
  direct template matching, 85
  dynamic programming, 85
  existing systems for, 86-87
  filtering, 84
  HARPY, 87
  Hear What I Mean (HWIM), 87
  HEARSAY, 87
  island driving, 86
  linear predictive analysis, 84
  Logos speech analyzer, 88
  Loops system, 88
  operation of, initial analysis, 84-85
  problems in, 83-84
  programming languages and, 120
  recent developments in, 88
  recognition techniques for, 85
  segmentation, 85, 86
  sound generation and, 83
  speech systems and research, 86
  USA, 18-19
  voice typewriter and, 88
  Voice-Operated Database Inquiry System (VODIS), 88
  zero-crossing count, 84
Speech Understanding Research (SUR), USA, 86
Sperry, 73
spherical coordinate robotics arm, 115
Spur RISC computer, 18
SRI International, 86, 165
SRL expert systems, 175, 176
Stanford Artificial Intelligence Language (SAIL), 141
Stanford University, 162, 164, 165, 166, 175
STC, 28, 30
STET, 25
Strategic Computing for Image Understanding (SCIUP), USA, 12, 20
Strategic Computing Initiative (SCI), 12, 62
  artificial vision and, 107
  Butterfly and, 17
  DARPA and, 12
  SDI and, 13
Strategic Defense Initiative (SDI), 13, 59, 68, 71
Strathclyde University, 29
Stuttgart University, 77
supercomputer (see Cray, Hypertron)
superconductivity, 59
  Josephson junction and, 73
Superspeed Computer Project, 4-5
superwafer (see wafer-scale integration)
SWIRL, 176
Synaptics, Inc., 105
syntax, natural languages, 146

Syntelligence, 176
System Building Aids, expert systems, 172
Systems Designers, 29

T

tactical evolution, Pilot's Associate and, 15
tape-automated bonding (TAB) process, 22
TEIRESIAS expert systems, 172, 175
Teknowledge, 176
Tektronix, 66
tetracyanoquinodimethane (TCNQ), 76, 77
tetrahiofulvalene (TTF), 76
Texas Instruments, 16, 18, 65, 66
text editors, 173
Thinking Machines Corporation, 17
Thomas J. Watson Research Center, 88, 105
Thomason-CSF, 25
threat assessment, Pilot's Associate, 14
Tokyo Institute of Technology, 68
toolkits, 28, 29, 30, 171-173, 176
Toshiba, 5, 65
transistor, optical, 69
transitional parsing, 147
transphasor, 58, 69-71
transputers, 29
TRW, 68, 73

U

United States fifth-generation technology research, 11-22
  Air-Land Battle Management System, 16
  architectures, 16-18
  Autonomous Land Vehicle, 15
  future projects, 16
  image analysis, 19
  industry research projects in, 20
  Japan and, 7
  Microcomputer and Computer Technology Corp., 20
  natural language recognition, 18
  optical interconnections, 19
  Pilot's Associate, 13-15
  Semiconductor Research Corporation, 22
  sensors research, 19
  speech recognition, 18-19
  Strategic Computing for Image Recognition, 12, 20
  Strategic Computing Initiative, 12
UNITS expert systems, 175
University College of London, 29
USSR and Eastern Europe fifth-generation technology research, 31-34
Utah University, 125

V

VDM Toolset, 28
vector processing, parallel processing and, 44-45
Velikhov, Yerengyi, 32
vision systems, 12, 91-107
  applications for, 93-95
  "block world" and, 102
  computer vision technology, 95-104
  controlled hallucination, 104
  edge detection, 98
  feature detectors, 105
  Gaussian filters, 99
  heterarchial constraint propagation, 103
  knowledge representation problems and, 102
  knowledge-directed vision, 96
  machine vision, 104-107
  optical illusions and, 100-101
  pattern recognition, 95, 96
  primal sketch, 97
  programming languages and, 120
  segmentation, 97
  signal processing for, 98
  versatility of vision and, 93
Vitesse Electronics, 66
VLSE, 7, 22
VLSI, 8, 21, 26, 27, 28, 29, 30, 60
  parallel processing and, 39
VM expert systems, 163, 175
voice print identification, speech recognition and, 81
voice typewriter, 88
voice-operated database inquiry (VODIS) speech recognition system, 88
voice-operated toys, speech recognition and, 81
von Neumann machines, 42, 43
von Neumann, John, 42, 43

W

wafer-scale integration, 64-66
Warwick University, 75
Weaver, Warren, 144
Wiesel, Torsten, 105
WILLARD expert systems, 167
Woods, William, 147

X

XCON expert systems, 165, 175, 175
Xerox, 68, 176
x-ray lithography, 39
XSEL expert systems, 175

Y

Yale University, 150, 152

Z

zero-crossing count, speech recognition and, 84

IONA COLLEGE
RYAN LIBRARY
715 NORTH AVENUE
NEW ROCHELLE, NY 10801

DATE			

© THE BAKER & TAYLOR CO.